TRACING YOUR
IRISH & BRITISH ROOTS

Volume VI of *Quillen's Essentials of Genealogy*

www.essentialgenealogy.com

PRAISE FOR DAN'S BOOKS

"Mastering Online Genealogy written by W. Daniel Quillen is a great little book packed full of helpful tips in doing online family research ... This informative book has some great tips for beginners, as well as those who have been doing research for a while ... I look forward to reading all of the books in this genealogical series." – *Tina Sansone, Bella Online book review*

"Your book *Secrets of Tracing your Ancestors* has been extremely helpful to me in a renewal of my genealogy interests." – *Nancy Dailey*

"I would like to thank you for writing a very informative book. There was a lot of information that I did not know about…" – *Donna Perryman Moon*

"I purchased your book and have found it most helpful." – *Glenda Laney*

"Thanks for your help and for writing your excellent book!" – *Laura Johnson*

"I have enjoyed reading your book and I've found excellent leads for finding ancestors." – *Donna Mann*

"… It is not only informative but entertaining. Incorporating your own experiences in brought the book to life. Again, thank you for helping me to understand the many aspects of genealogy and for supplying a roadmap to finding more information about our ancestors." – *Dana L. Hager*

"Of all the books I have looked at yours is the best…and you write with your heart and soul. Thanks for writing such a great book." – *Karen Dredge*

"I got this book out of the library, but before I was half-way through it, I decided I had to have my own copy. Lots of helpful suggestions! I'd recommend it for all new and experienced family historians." – *Margaret Combs*

"I am embarking on the family history journey and have found your book to be very helpful … thanks for putting together a helpful, easy to follow guide." – *Suzanne Adams*

"I'm absolutely delighted that I discovered your book "Secrets of Tracing Your Ancestors." I've only been at this for a month (to keep sane during knee surgery recuperation) and now I'm hooked." – *Cecily Bishop*

About the Author

For more than 20 years, W. Daniel Quillen has been a professional writer specializing in travel and technical subjects. He has taught beginning genealogy courses to university students and working adults, and is a frequent lecturer in beginning and intermediate genealogy classes in Colorado. He has compiled his years of genealogical training and research into a growing series of genealogy how-to books. He lives in Centennial, Colorado with his wife and children. If you would like to contact Dan about anything in this book, his e-mail address is: **wdanielquillen@gmail.com**.

TRACING YOUR
IRISH & BRITISH ROOTS

Volume VI of *Quillen's Essentials of Genealogy*

www.essentialgenealogy.com

W. Daniel Quillen

Author of *Secrets of Tracing Your Ancestors*; *The Troubleshooter's Guide to Do-It-Yourself Genealogy*; and *Quillen's Essentials of Genealogy* books, a new series of genealogy primers

Cold Spring Press

COLD SPRING PRESS

P.O. Box 284
Cold Spring Harbor, NY 11724
E-mail: jopenroad@aol.com
www.essentialgenealogy.com

ISBN 10: 1-59360-156-0
ISBN 13: 978-159360-156-5
Library of Congress Control Number: 2012936569

PHOTO CREDITS

From flickr.com: front cover: Images of History; back cover: Greene Connections; page 7: T"eresa; page 11: AVASKEG (David); pages 83, 131: Playingwithbrushes Photos on page 132 courtesy of W. Daniel Quillen.

Cover design by Matthew Simmons (www.myselfincluded.com).

If you want to contact the author directly, e-mail him at: wdanielquillen@gmail.com

TABLE OF CONTENTS

2662

1. INTRODUCTION

Welcome! Welcome to *Tracing Your Irish & British Roots*. America has been the destination for Irish and British immigrants since long before her establishment as a country several centuries ago. In fact, my first ancestor to come to America was Teague McQuillan, who arrived in Jamestown in 1635, nearly 140 years before the Revolutionary War.

The 2010 Census tells this tale of the population in the United States, as Americans identified their ancestry as:

Irish	34,670,009 (11.2%)
English / British	25,927,345 (8.3%)
Scottish	5,460,679 (1.8%)
Scottish-Irish	3,257,161 (1.1%)
Total	70,496,751 (22.8%)

The ancestors of over seventy million Americans hail from two islands off the west coast of Europe, islands that are roughly the size of Indiana (Ireland and Northern Ireland) and Kansas (England and Scotland), respectively. Nearly one in four Americans identified ancestors from one or both of these two islands in the 2010 census. One in four.

Since you picked up this book (thank you!), chances are your ancestors come from one or more of those islands. Through the pages of this book, we'll investigate some of the places you can go to unearth (no pun intended – well, maybe a little) your Irish and British ancestors' records.

Quillen's Essentials of Genealogy: Tracing Your Irish and British Roots is the fifth in a series of other *Quillen's Essentials* books. One or more of the others may come in handy for your ancestral research:

- *Quillen's Essentials of Genealogy: Mastering Online Genealogy*
- *Quillen's Essentials of Genealogy: Mastering Immigration and Naturalization Records*
- *Quillen's Essentials of Genealogy: Mastering Census and Military Records*
- *Quillen's Essentials of Genealogy: Tracing Your European Roots*
- *Quillen's Essentials of Genealogy: Tracing Your Irish & British Roots*
- *Quillen's Essentials of Genealogy: Mastering Family, Library and Church Records (coming soon)*

While each of those books represents a focused dive into various areas of genealogical research, one of the first two genealogy books I wrote might also prove useful to you:

Secrets of Tracing Your Ancestors – This book was originally targeted at beginning genealogists, although reviewers have noted it contains sections, topics and tactics that are beneficial to beginning as well as more experienced researchers.

Troubleshooter's Guide to Do-It-Yourself Genealogy – This book is designed for genealogists with a little more experience in genealogical research, or perhaps those who have hit brick walls in their research and need a little extra help.

Cold Spring Press publishes all the books in *The Quillen's Essentials of Genealogy* series as well as *Secrets* and the *Troubleshooter's Guide.*

As you explore your Irish and/or British Roots, if you run into difficulties, have questions, or just want to bounce something off me, you are welcome to e-mail me at *wdanielquillen@gmail.com.*

Now that the shameless self-promotion is out of the way, we can get down to finding your Irish and British ancestors. However, before we jump into the records, let's talk about *The Basics* of searching for your Irish and British ancestors.

2. THE BASICS

Before you begin your cross-oceanic search for your Irish and British ancestors, there are some research basics you should keep in mind. In *Secrets of Tracing Your Ancestors*, I spend a good deal of time encouraging my readers to begin their genealogical research with the information they have at hand. What do your parents, grandparents, aunts, uncles and cousins know about the ancestor you are researching? Can they shed some light on the Irish county or town your ancestor called home before coming to America? It would be well for you to glean every bit of that information they have about your ancestors. Be cautious with this information (because some of it may be inaccurate!), but seek and record as much as possible.

For researching my Irish and British ancestors, find out what my family members may already know!

Do any of your relatives have documents from your ancestors that may assist you? A birth certificate of your grandmother may tell you not only when and where she was born, but it may also tell you who her parents were (including her mother's maiden name), as well as their birth places.

A marriage license for one of your ancestors who immigrated to America may provide a town or other geographic clue as to where she and her husband were married, and perhaps where they were born (people weren't as mobile as our society is today – they and their ancestors often lived and died within a very small geographic area).

See if you can glean the following information:

•Surname(s) of the individual(s) you are researching;
•Names of parents, siblings, spouses (including maiden names of women), etc.;
•County where they came from;
•Town, city, parish, province, region, etc. they lived in;
•Approximate years of critical events such as births, marriages and deaths

Patronymics

Since we are researching Irish and British roots, it is valuable for us to spend a short amount of time on patronymics – the practice of the Irish in particular to use a name that identifies the named person with his or her father.

The Irish had their own form of patronymics recognized the world over. Prefixes such as Mc or Mac were used to signify the *son of*: McDonnell was therefore the son of Donnell. Another prefix was the O' which meant "descended from," and a grandson or great grandson might use such a prefix. Occasionally the English passed laws to annoy the Irish (actually, they were trying to assimilate them into English culture). One such law forbade the use of the patronymics *O* and *Mc*. At that time, the French patronymic *fitz* replaced *Mc* for son of: Fitzmorris then meant the son of Morris.

The Irish and British also – primarily in generations past – used a naming pattern for their sons and daughters. Typically, it was:

• The first son was named after the father's father
• The second son was named after the mother's father
• The third son was named after the father

- The fourth son was named after the father's eldest brother
- The fifth son was named after the mother's eldest brother
- The first daughter was named after the mother's mother
- The second daughter was named after the father's mother
- The third daughter was named after the mother
- The fourth daughter was named after the mother's eldest sister
- The fifth daughter was named after the father's eldest sister

These naming patterns were most common between the early 1700s and the latter end of the 1800s. While they weren't always cast in stone, they very often followed this pattern. Something good to be aware of.

Spelling Woes

Here's a hint that is probably heresy to my 6th grade teacher: Don't limit yourself to only one spelling of your name. In my research, in nearly every one of my family lines, at one time or another I have found variations in the

---

DON'T DO IT!

I can almost guarantee you that at some time or other in your research you will run across information that you'll "know" just isn't right. The temptation will be to correct the information rather than just write down what you have found.

Don't do it!

Perhaps it's the first name of an ancestor. While you might be absolutely certain that your great-great grandmother's name is Theodora, if you find her listed in a US Census as "Dolly," that is the name you should record as you copy the data down. Or perhaps it's your last name that has been spelled creatively. Resist the temptation to substitute the information that is different. Copy the record exactly as you find it so that you can have an accurate representation of what you found.

---

spelling – sometimes within the same generation! Here are a few examples from my own family:

•Sellers, Sellars, Sellar
•Ritchie, Ritchey, Richey
•Horney, Harney
•Quillan, Quillen, Quillon, Quillin, McQuillan, McQuillon, etc.
•Lowrance/Lorentz
•McCollough/McCullough
•Rogers/Rodgers
•Throckmorton, Throgmorton
•Hudson/Hutson
•Graham/Grimes

Be open to a variety of spellings of family names.

And just because you are a Smith or a Jones (by the way — is it true that the surname of Adam and Eve was Jones?), don't assume you are immune from spelling changes: Smith / Smythe / Smithy / Schmidt or Jones / Jonas/ Joans, etc.

I have a very fresh example of the need to be open to name variations. As I was writing this book, I was in correspondence with a niece of mine who was researching her father's family, a group of Germans who settled in Russia near the Volga River. Her maiden name is Behm, and she discovered that the German name *Böhm* was often spelled *Boehm*, and the variation of *Behm* from *Boehm* was not a far-fetched idea. All this she accepted. There were no online or microfilm census records for the areas where her relatives lived, but through a lot of digging on the Internet, she found a source that was selling copies of the 1832 and 1864 censuses that would have included the Volga River German enclave her ancestors were a part of. She talked her father and sister into splitting the cost of the censuses and she ordered them.

She was so excited to search the censuses for her ancestor Henry Behm / Boehm / Böhm. The day came that the census arrived, and she feverishly checked the families and was at first delighted to see many Böhm families. But – alas, there was not one single Henry among them. She was heartbroken and distraught. My sister shared her frustrations – there were plenty of Heinrichs, but not a single Henry! I gently pointed out that in 1832 Germany there probably wouldn't have been anyone named Henry – they would have only been named *Heinrich*! Joy returned to my niece and her family.

I have a similar situation in my own family. The McQuillan Clan, of which I am a part, were fairly important in the annals of the northern part of Ireland. In fact, there have been fairly accurate genealogies kept of them back to medieval times – the fourth century AD, to be precise. But there were not McQuillans or even McQuillins back then. We seem to have been descended from a fellow named Niall Mag Uillin. It's easy to see how the name evolved through the years from Mag Uillin to McQuillin.

There are many reasons for variation of name spellings, and your creative detective work will have to gather all the threads together into one cohesive answer. Immigration officials are often accused of this, but in my opinion that happened far less than was alleged. The name change may have been due to an immigration official, or it may have been illiteracy. Another reason might be that the newly immigrated family wanted to fit in to their new country. In that case, Meier became Meyer, Schneider became Snider, Schmidt became Smith and Blau became Blue. In my family, McQuillan became Quillan, which became (for my line of the family) Quillen.

Before we get too far along this genealogical journey we're taking together, let's take a few minutes and set the stage for searching for your Irish and British ancestors. There are many records available to assist your research.

I have found that it usually takes multiple records to yield the information I am looking for. One document sheds light in one area, which leads me to another, which confirms the previous data and provides me with more data. Tiny clues are hidden in records, clues that initially may not seem to be important, but which may later prove to be just the item of information needed to solve a mystery.

The goal, of course, is to find the genealogical information for an ancestor and their family. As you discover a birth date and birth place in records closer to home (immigration or census records, for example), those will lead you to the land of nativity for your ancestor, and perhaps even to their home town or parish. Further searches in the land of their nativity will likely confirm information reported on the immigration or naturalization record, uncover other family members, and assist you in moving further along on your pedigree chart, pushing it ever up the family tree, further and further back in time.

To be the most efficient in your search, first gather all the information you know about your ancestor. Speak with parents, grandparents, aunts and uncles, cousins, etc. One of them may recall information that will become important to your search. Maybe they recalled that their grandfather mentioned how beautiful Boston was when he stepped off the ship in America. Or perhaps they remember that great grandpa quipped that he had two quid in his pockets when he stepped off the ship in America.

United States records first. Often, information that will help you in your search for immigrant ancestors will be information found in United States records. A census record that lists your ancestor may list him or her under a name you didn't realize they went by. As an example, the 1920 census lists my great grandmother as Dolly. Her full name was Theodora Charity McCollough, but the name she went by was Dolly. So a search of a census, immigration or naturalization record might not turn her up if you search for Theodora Charity McCollough Quillen. At a minimum, I should search under Theodora, Charity and Dolly. A death certificate, tombstone, obituary or other very US record may well reveal information I did not know, but information that will help me pinpoint her later on in other records.

What's in a name? Further to the discussion above — do you know your ancestors' given as well as surnames? Knowing their given names – all of them – may help you sort out your ancestor from millions of others. Perhaps he or she went by their middle or christening name. While you might be unable to locate your ancestor Patrick McQuillan in records, you might discover a Teague McQuillan who immigrated to the United States. Patrick Teague McQuillan, like the author of this book, just happened to go by his middle name, not his first name.

As mentioned above in the example about my great grandmother, Theodora Charity Quillen, as I scour records in search of her, I'd do well to be open to diminutives (Timmy for Tim, Billy or Willy for William, Paddy for Patrick, etc.) as well as other possible nicknames.

Know your history. Knowing a little of the history of your family as well as their native country may also help you pin down that immigrant ancestor of yours. If family tradition is that your second great grandfather came to America during the *Great Potato Famine* in Ireland, then that narrows your search for other records to a manageable half dozen years or so – 1845 to 1852. During that time period, blight hit the potatoes of Ireland, rotting them in the ground. Potatoes were the main staple for the Irish diet, and it is estimated that approximately one million souls perished as a result of the famine. In addition, approximately another million Irish emigrated from Ireland during this time, the majority of which came to America. If your grandmother tells you that her grandfather came to America to flee the Great Potato Famine, you'll have a good idea when he left the Emerald Isle. If she further tells you that he was a teenager when he came to America, you can place his birth date someplace between about 1826 and 1838 – the span of years he would have been a teenager during the Great Potato Famine.

One of my wife's ancestors is from Germany. Family tradition holds that as it looked like Germany was headed into what has become known as The Great War (World War I), her second great grandmother packed her four military-age sons off to America to get them out of harm's way. That tells me I should search for their immigration records in the years leading up to the war's outbreak in 1914.

So – pay attention to history!

Ethnic gatherings. Often, immigrants coming to America were coming to join other family members or neighbors. As you search for your immigrant ancestors, be aware of where large populations of their ethnic group may have settled. Swedes ended up in Minnesota, the Irish centered in Boston and New York, the Polish in Chicago, Italians in New York and Chicago, even Bulgarians in New Mexico. (Bet you didn't know that!) While stereotypes or assumptions such as these may not apply to your ancestors, you cannot afford to overlook the possibility. Had I Irish ancestors (I do – lucky me!), I would be sure and search immigration records for Boston and New York. Could they have entered the US someplace else? Of course. But as a starting point, these ports of entry make the most sense if I have nothing better to go on.

Religion. You ask why religious affiliation should be considered? Well, because sometimes like-minded religionists immigrated to the US at the same time. Look at the founding of our country, which started with a colony of Pilgrims who came to America aboard the Mayflower, followed by the Puritans. Many early Pennsylvania pioneers were Quakers. If your ancestors came from Ireland, they're sure to be Catholic, right? Well, maybe – remember that the area that is now Northern Ireland was once "planted" by the Queen Elizabeth with Protestants during the late 16th and 17th centuries (there's that history thing again!). Searching Catholic baptismal records for an ancestor from the six northern counties of Ireland might prove fruitless.

Well, that's it – I've set the stage, and we're ready to jump off in search of your Irish / British ancestors.

Do I know my ancestors' religious preferences? That may help.

3. TRACING YOUR IRISH ROOTS

We have always found the Irish a bit odd. They refuse to be English. — Winston Churchill

Cead mille failte! — Gaelic (Irish) greeting meaning: one hundred thousand welcomes!

Welcome to the world of Irish research.

Through the years, I have had a lot of fun (and not a little frustration!) searching for my Irish ancestors. On one hand, my Irish ancestors have made it relatively easy on me – almost all of my Irish direct lines (nine at last count: Graham, Grimes, Lindsay, McCollough, McQuillan, Peoples, Sellers, Ritchie, and Rodgers) came to America in the 1600s and 1700s. Some started in Scotland (McCollough and Lindsay, at least), stopping in Ireland for varying lengths of time (usually several generations) before coming to America. Either way, by the time I leaped over the Atlantic to do research on those lines, I was well back in time, where records were a little more difficult to find.

If you have read any of my other genealogy books (or even if you've read the first chapter of this book!), you'll know what my counsel will be: find everything you can here in the good ol' United States. We'll discuss US records that will assist in finding your Irish ancestors, even in Ireland.

Family Tradition / Legend / Knowledge

Before you venture too far – see what family members know about your Irish ancestors. Often, extended family members – grandparents, aunts and uncles, cousins, etc, may hold the key to finding more about your Irish ancestors. They may know where they came from in Ireland, may know about the time they came here ("Well, grandpa always said he was five years old when he stepped off the boat in Boston,"), and where they arrived. These last two items of information – when and where they arrived – are keys to finding other records that may lead you to the very town in Ireland from which your ancestors hailed.

As you glean your information, be careful with the information. First – write it down. Second – use it as a guide, but not the Gospel truth. I learned that lesson the hard way. My great grandmother kept a genealogy for several generations beyond her and her husband which reached back to the 1700s. She identified one of her huband's ancestors as Scottish. Well, I took her at her word, and spent a great deal of time scouring Scottish records in search of that elusive ancestor. I eventually found her in Ireland – not Scotland. That is typical, by the way – the Irish and Scots frequently jumped over the long and slender Irish Sea to marry, work, raid, etc. So if you have Irish ancestors, be sure and allow for the possibility they came from Scotland. Conversely, if you have Scottish ancestors, you may find their birth and marriage information in Ireland or England.

Census records

The federal censuses for 1900, 1910, 1920, 1930 and 1940 each asks a series of questions that may provide clues that will assist you in finding these Irish ancestors of yours. These censuses all asked whether a person had been naturalized, along with other helpful immigration-related questions. The 1920 census went a step further by requesting the year of naturalization. That last will be especially helpful, and will assist you in locating your ancestor's naturalization papers. By census, here are the immigration and naturalization questions asked (this is in addition to the questions that asked for the birth place of the individual and of his and her parents):

1900
- If an immigrant, the year of immigration to the United States
- How long the immigrant has been in the United States
- Is the person naturalized?

1910
- Year of immigration to the United States
- Whether naturalized or alien
- Whether able to speak English, or, if not, give language spoken

1920
- Year of immigration to the United States
- Naturalized or alien
- If naturalized, year of naturalization

1930
- Year of immigration into the United States
- Naturalization
- Whether able to speak English

1940
- Citizenship of the foreign born
- Mother tongue (or native language) if foreign born
- Citizenship of the foreign born?

In the *Citizenship* column of these censuses, where the above questions were asked, these abbreviations were used: AL = Alien, NA = Naturalized, NR =

Not Reported, PA = First Papers filed (the immigrant's declaration of intention).

As you review this information, you will be able to determine if indeed your ancestor was born in Ireland (or elsewhere). Pay particular attention to the abbreviations used in the Citizenship column; you are particularly hopeful that you find one of the following in that column for your ancestor:

- NA = Naturalized
- PA = First Papers

Naturalized means that your ancestor may have gone through the process of completing the naturalization process. The application (called Petition for Citizenship), often had a great deal of genealogical information contained in it about the individual and his/her family. I say *may* have gone through the process, since before 1922, women received citizenship by virtue of their husband's citizenship, whether naturalized or already an American citizen. Also, minor children received citizenship by virtue of their father's citizenship. So even though the census indicates a female ancestor may have been naturalized, she may not have completed any paperwork. Same with her minor children.

First papers means the immigrant had filed his first immigration papers, also known as *Declarations of Intention*. These papers were frequently filed within days of an immigrant's arrival in America. Often, however, they were not followed up on – their naturalization wasn't completed. But that's okay — even Declarations of Intention have excellent genealogical data available on them.

First papers = Declaration of Intention to immigrate. Great genealogy information!

Let me introduce you to a long-lost cousin of mine – Frederick John McQuillan, who was an Irish immigrant to the United States. I will use him and some of his family members to illustrate some of the search techniques and tactics you can use to find your Irish ancestors.

Fred first appears as a boarder with the John and Margaret Hanratty family in New York City in the 1920 census:

Name	Age	Year Immigrated	Naturalized or Alien?	Year Naturalized
Hanratty, John	42	1906	NA	1913
Margaret	34	1905	NA	
McQuillan, Fred	28	1915	AL	

The record also indicated Fred was an iron worker in a shipyard. This is a very typical entry in census records in the late 19th, early 20th centuries. Often, Irish men came to America ahead of their families to establish a foothold, and test the waters so to speak – could they get work, what were the living conditions like? Could they support their family if they brought them over?

Often, these men would live in boarding houses, or if they were fortunate, with friends or family. I should watch for other records that might identify whether or not John or Margaret Hanratty is a relative.

I decided to check the 1930 census for the Hanrattys, just to have any additional information about this family in my back pocket. My first thought is that Margaret may be Fred's sister or perhaps his aunt, but I still have a long way to go to prove that! Here's what I found for the John Hanratty family in the 1930 census:

Name	Age	Year Immigrated	Naturalized or Alien?	Age at First Marriage
Hanratty, John	50	1906	NA	30
Margaret	48	1906	NA	28

It's interesting to note that between 1920 and 1930, John aged only eight years (what a great country!), but Margaret aged fourteen years (yikes!). Such are the vagaries of the census records sometimes. Their dates of immigration would indicate this is likely the same couple, despite the fact their ages don't match up exactly. The 1930 entry also tells us that John was born in the Irish Free State (The Republic of Ireland), as were his parents, and Margaret was born in Northern Ireland, as were her parents.

I also thought I would see if I could find Fred in the 1930 census. A few clicks of the mouse on Ancestry.com and I find the following family:

Name	Age	Age at First Marriage
McQuillan, Fred	36	26
Catherine	30	21

Year of Immigration	Place of Birth	Status of Naturalization
(Fred) 1914	Irish Free State	NA
(Catherine) 1929	Irish Free State	NA

So it looks like Fred stuck around for awhile. Since the 1920 census, Fred, like John, has only aged eight years, and he is now a naturalized citizen. His wife, Catherine, immigrated to the US in 1929, but is already a naturalized citizen, most likely as a result of her husband's naturalization. It seems curious, however, that Fred and Catherine were married approximately nine years before this census was taken, yet, Catherine didn't immigrate to the United States until the previous year. Also, Fred was listed on the 1920

census as having immigrated in 1915, but
on this census, he is listed as having immigrated in 1914. Memories do dim, or who-
ever provided the information (in this case,
probably Catherine), may not have known
for certain and estimated.

Irish Free State =
Republic of Ireland

Note the place of birth for both Fred and
Catherine is listed as *Irish Free State*. This is in reference to the 1922 Treaty
that separated Northern Ireland from the rest of Ireland. The Irish Free
State is the same as today's Republic of Ireland.

Immigration Records

When I write about *immigration* records, I am referring to those records that
detail information about your ancestors' trip (immigration) to America.
They include:

1. **Ship passenger lists** – these are the rosters of all who traveled on a
   particular ship to the United States. They are sometimes called ship
   manifests. These records, especially in later immigration years,
   contain a great deal of information of genealogical value.

2. **Certificates of arrival** – these were short notices containing the
   immigrant's name, date of departure and arrival, port of departure
   and entry and the name of the ship on which they traveled. Very
   little information of genealogical value is to be found on Certificates
   of Arrival, but they may lead you to other more helpful documents.

3. **Censuses** – censuses taken in later years after an immigrants' arrival
   may contain valuable clues to finding immigration and
   naturalization papers completed by the immigrant. The census

itself is full of genealogical value, but may lead you to other documents that will expand that information exponentially.

4. **Emigration records** – these are records kept at the location where your ancestor embarked on a ship to come to America. Sometimes they provide significant information, sometimes they do not. Don't overlook them when searching for your immigrant ancestors.

When I write about *naturalization* records, I am referring to those records immigrants completed to become US citizens. There are several:

5. **Declarations of Intention** – these were papers completed to indicate the immigrant's intention to become a US citizen. They were often completed immediately upon arrival in the United States, but were sometimes completed later. These are often called first papers. These papers usually have a great deal of genealogical information in them.

6. **Petitions for Naturalization** – these papers were completed by the immigrant as part of his or her formal request to become a US citizen. Generally speaking, these could not be completed until an immigrant had been in the US at least five years. Also called second papers or final papers, as well as Petition for Citizenship. These papers usually have a great deal of genealogical information in them.

7. **Oaths of Allegiance** – this is the document the immigrant signs as s/he becomes a US citizen, renouncing his allegiance to any other foreign power, dignitary, king, etc. Very little information of genealogical value is contained in Oaths of Allegiance, but there may be some clues that will lead you to other sources of information.

Passenger Lists. One of my favorite sets of immigration records are passenger lists – also called *ship's manifests*. Of course, you have heard of Ellis Island (known as *Isola della Lacrime* – The Island of Tears — by Italian immigrants) – most genealogists have. But Ellis Island was only one of many ports of entry for immigrants arriving in the US. While more than 22,500,000 immigrants had Ellis Island as their first port of call in America, that leaves over three times that number to have come to American shores through other ports of entry. In fact, the US government officially took over the tracking of immigrants in 1890; prior to that, the states were responsible for tracking immigrants. As you can imagine, the information and rigor varied state-by-state, and administration-by-administration within those states. Some kept very good records and asked many questions, others kept scanty records with very little information beyond the name of the immigrant and date he or she passed through the port.

Between 1820 and 1920, immigrants entered the US in the following numbers at the following points:

Baltimore, MD – 1,460,000
Boston, MA — 2,050,000
Charleston, SC – 20,000
Galveston, TX – 110,000
Key West, FL – 130,000
New Bedford, MA – 40,000
New York City, NY – 32,500,000*
New Orleans, LA – 710,000
Passamaquoddy, Maine – 80,000
Philadelphia, PA – 1,240,000
Portland / Falmouth, ME – 120,000
Providence, RI – 40,000
San Francisco, CA – 500,000

* — Castle Garden, the predecessor to Ellis Island, was the first point of arrival for 10,000,000 immigrants between 1830 and 1892, the year that Ellis Island opened.

As you can see, the top ports in order of numbers of immigrants processed in the United States were:

New York
Boston
Baltimore
Philadelphia
New Orleans
San Francisco

Passenger lists may provide significant genealogical data!

If you are looking for Irish immigrants, you might focus first on New York, Boston, Philadelphia and Baltimore. There are several reasons for this:
- between those four ports, nearly 39 million immigrants arrived;
- there are significant Irish enclaves in and around those cities;
- those four ports represented more-or-less straight shots from the ports from which the Irish were most likely to have left.

Based on the 1920 census, Fred McQuillan immigrated in 1915. During the 1920 census he was living in New York City, so I will focus on the New York port to see if I can find Fred on a passenger list, arriving from Ireland. As stated before, Castle Garden operated between 1830 and 1892, and Ellis Island operated between 1892 and 1924, so that's a good place for me to search for Fred. Since Ellis Island has one of the premier websites for searching passenger lists, let me give you a little more information on it.

Ellis Island website. If your ancestors came to America between 1892 and 1924, you'll definitely want to check out *www.ellisisland.org*, the official website for that immigration gateway into the United States. During that time, more than 22.5 million individuals were processed through her gates, all headed for the freedoms America offered. Before you can do much on the website, you must register. This is a relatively painless (and free) process that takes all of one or two minutes. Once registered, you'll be able to tour around and see most of the information available on the website.

The most robust feature of the website is the *Passenger Search*, which allows you to search for your ancestor among the 12 million passengers whose names were on passenger lists of ships that arrived at Ellis Island. These individuals may have been passengers, immigrants or crew members who arrived in America between 1892 and 1924. Volunteers spent years microfilming, transcribing, cataloging and indexing the information for the Ellis Island Foundation. And now the information is available to you.

Getting information from the website is quite easy. From the home page of *www.ellisisland.org*, click on *Passenger Search*, and then click on *New Search* on the page that appears. On the next page, type the first and last names (at least the last name) of the ancestor you are looking for, indicate whether they are male or female, and then click on *Start search*. In this case, we'll type Fred McQuillan. I also enter his approximate date of birth. From the 1930 census, I estimate that to be about 1892, since he was 28 years old on the 1920 census.

Immediately I am greeted with a hit:

Name	Residence	Arrived	Age on Arrival
Frederick John			
McQuillan	Crossmaglen, Ireland	1915	23

This looks like it could be the Fred I am seeking. Recall the 1920 census says he arrived in 1915, and that he was 28 years old in 1920. This entry correlates with that information.

This is the first time I learn that his name is Frederick John McQuillan – if indeed I have the correct Fred McQuillan.

If I click on that record, I am taken to an image that looks like a certificate in a frame. It transcribes some of the information from the passenger list – his name, age at arrival, date of arrival and the ship on which he traveled. While that is interesting, I really want to take a look at the actual ship's manifest (passenger list). So, at the top of that page, click on *Original Ship Manifest*. You'll be taken to a page that is much too small to read. Don't panic – look for the small magnifying glass icon (just above and to the right of the image of the passenger list) and click on it.

You'll immediately see a large version of the actual image of the passenger list. On Ellis Island's website, sometimes it seems you've entered the second page of the passenger list, since it begins in column 12, and at the left side of the image there is no name. In this instance, that's exactly what's happened – you have entered on the second page of the manifest. (In later years, ship's manifests were in a large log book which covered two facing pages.) To get to the first page, close the window (top right-hand corner); this will return you to the small image of the manifest. Near the magnifying glass icon, you'll see the page number, and the opportunity to go to the previous page. Click on *previous*, and you'll be on the first page of the manifest.

Voila! On the second line you'll see the name of Frederick John McQuillan. Here is the information contained on both pages of the manifest (you'll need to close this page again and reopen the second page):

Name: Frederick John McQuillan
Sex: Male
Married or Single: Single
Occupation: Laborer
Nationality: British
Race or People: Irish
Residence: Crossmaglen, Ireland
Name and address of nearest relative or friend from home country: Felix
McQuillan, father, Dundalk, Ireland

Second page:

Final destination: New York
Name of relative or friend that will be visited: Niece – Jane Lynch, 1552
Broadway, New York
Height: 5'9"
Complexion, hair, eyes: dark, brown, blue
Born: Dundalk, Ireland

Wow – look at the genealogical information we were able to glean about
Frederick John McQuillan! We have his age (23 in 1915, so approximate
birth year of 1892), birth place (Dundalk, Ireland), father's name (Felix
McQuillan), and as an added bonus, we have the name of his niece – Jane
Lynch.

> **History.** Now – a little reminder about history. At the time of
> Fred's crossing to America, Ireland was still occupied by Britain –
> thus his identification as a British national, while his race / people
> was entered as Irish. The Irish were nearing freedom for most of the
> country, but that wasn't to happen until 1921. It is further
> interesting to note that his residence was Crossmaglen, Ireland,
> and his birth place is eleven miles away in Dundalk, Ireland. When

Northern Ireland is formed in 1921, Crossmaglen will be in the North, and Dundalk will remain in the Republic of Ireland.

I was also able to find a transcription of this record on *FamilySearch.org*. It provided a link to *www.ellisisland.org* for viewing the online image.

Just for grins, I decided to see if there were any other travel records for Fred. This time, I went to Ancestry.com and under the *Immigration and Travel Records* section, searched for Fred McQuillan. The search turned up an additional passenger record:

Fred McQuillan, age 46. Naturalized in the District Court of New York on June 20, 1927.

Fred had sailed from Cobh, Ireland on April 3, 1937 on the ship President Roosevelt, arriving in New York on April 10, 1937. (By the way – Cobh is a beautiful town on the southern coast of Ireland. It was the last Irish land many an Irish immigrant stepped off of, never to return. It was also the last port of call for the Titanic prior to her ill-fated push toward America.)

This is tremendous information! With the above information, perhaps I can find his naturalization papers, which should provide me with more important genealogical information for him and his family.

Naturalization records
In our search for information about Frederick John McQuillan, it's now time to search for his naturalization paperwork. The 1920 census, where he is living with the Hanratty family, says that Fred is an Alien – so he hadn't become a citizen at that time.

There are two basic naturalization records that are generally of great genealogical value – *Declarations of Intention*, and *Petition for Citizenship*. The first typically is filed shortly upon the immigrant's arrival in the United States, while the second is filed at the time the immigrant wants to apply for citizenship – usually no sooner than five years after arrival.

The 1920 census record for Fred provides some interesting information regarding naturalization that may not be immediately obvious. As mentioned a few paragraphs above, Fred is listed as an Alien (AL). However, if true, that means that even though Fred had arrived in America in 1915, he had still not filed a Declaration of Intention. Had he done so, the census entry would have been PA – meaning first papers (Declaration of Intention) had been filed. So, even though Fred had been in the United States since 1915, he had not yet declared his intent to become a US citizen. Unless – and this is always a possibility – unless the person who was providing the information (likely Margaret Hanratty) was unaware that he had filed his first papers.

I first went to Ancestry.com in search of Fred's Declaration of Intention, and found his name in an index of Declarations…but his specific Declaration of Intention is apparently not yet online. I checked several other sources: Fold3 (formerly *www.Footnote.com*), Archive.com, the National Archives and Records Administration website (*www.archives.gov*) and *FamilySearch.org*, and was not able to locate an online image of his Declaration of Intention.

Since it appears Fred's Declaration of Intention isn't yet online, I turned my attention to finding his Petition for Citizenship, and found success. Ancestry.com had Fred's petition, and here is the information I found on Fred:

Name: Frederick John McQuillan
Birth date: August 25, 1891
Birth place: Dundalk, Ireland

Place of residence: 301 East 33rd Street, New York City

Occupation: Riveter

Arrived: September 2, 1915 on the St. Paul

Wife's name: Catherine McQuillan

Wife's birth date: December 18, 1899

Wife's birthplace: Ireland

Children's names and birth dates:

      Patrick, April 15, 1921, born Ireland

      Margaret, May 23, 1923, born Ireland

Residence of children and wife: Ireland

Military service: entered service on December 7, 1917, received honorable discharge on June 5, 1919. Service number: 1710687

Fred's naturalization papers were witnessed by Margaret Hanratty of 325 East 33rd Street – which means she was living a few doors down from Fred.

> Try to find naturalization records for my ancestors – lots of genealogical information there!

If you'll recall, we found Fred living with John and Margaret Hanratty on the 1920 Census for New York City. Fred's Petition for Citizenship was completed in 1927, so Fred stayed in the same neighborhood. Again, a couple more hints that Fred and Margaret may be related.

Passport Applications

As we've seen with Frederick John McQuillan, immigrants to the United States often traveled back and forth between the US and their native countries. (We've identified two crossings for him so far.) Many, perhaps most, immigrants left significant portions of their families behind as they headed for the Promised Land that was America. Aging (or not so aging) parents, grandparents, siblings, and sometimes even spouses and children were left behind.

I have reviewed many passport applications that listed as a reason for the return to the immigrant's native land things like:
— returning to settle an estate
— returning to close out a business
— returning to sell my farm

And so on – in addition to family members to visit, lives were left behind and things still needed attending to.

And don't forget – their native homeland represented a tempting destination for those who were able to make their fortune (or at least a living) in America, and they wanted to return to the home country for a vacation and visit. For example, it is interesting to note that even today, it is estimated that 70% of American travelers to Ireland have Irish ancestors. I have made that pilgrimage, even though most of my ancestors, and especially my McQuillan ancestors, have been in America for several hundred years. There is just an irresistible draw to the home country for many. How much more so for those who themselves left that cherished homeland!?

As with so many of the other immigration and naturalization records we have discussed, the questions asked of those making application for a passport varied throughout the history of our country. Passports were not required until 1941; prior to that they were available and recommended, but not re-

> **Immigrant ancestors traveled back to their native land for a variety of reasons.**

quired (except for brief periods during the Civil War and World War I). Even at that, the National Archives has nearly two million passport applications on file for travelers between 1795 and 1925. The applications for these passports sometimes provide genealogical information.

Until the first quarter of the 20th century, the vast majority of passports (95%) were issued to men. This doesn't mean women didn't travel abroad; until the 1920s, women and children traveling with their husbands were listed on their husband's passport.

Unlike today's passports that are good for ten years (for adults), passports in the early years of the United States were valid for two years; therefore, you may find numerous passports for your ancestors.

The information found on passport applications varied through the years, but at a minimum they usually listed at least the full name, birth date and birth place of the individual. Many provided the physical description, which though not particularly of genealogical value, provide an interesting glimpse of an ancestor whom you would otherwise have no way of knowing what he or she looked like.

Histories / Biographies

In the latter half of the 19th century and the beginning of the 20th, city, county and even state histories were popular. An important part of these histories was the biography of the county's/ city's/ town's "leading citizens." Often, these biographies will shed tremendous light on your ancestors.

Before I go further, let me explain that *leading citizens* may have been some of the city's or county's oldest residents – their pioneers, if you will. They may have been those active in politics – mayors, governors, etc. Or simply those who were willing to pay a small fee to have their story told in the pages of the book. These latter biographical subjects may have been every-day people: farmers, dairy men, blacksmiths or store keepers.

I checked to see if I could find any biographies for cousin Fred, and wasn't able to come up with anything. But to share an example of what such a biography looks like, following is a short excerpt about a neighbor of my fourth great grandfather's, whose life was captured in *Biographies of Old Schuyler County (Illinois) Settlers*, written in 1878:

WILLIAM DEAN

William Dean was born in County Dennygaul, Ireland, May 3d, 1825, and is a son of John Dean. He received his early education in the district schools of Ireland. At about the age of twenty-two he immigrated to America, landing in New York. From there he went to the western part of Pennsylvania, where he resided two years. He then moved to Schuyler County, Illinois, in the spring of 1850, where he engaged in farming. In March, 1857, he was married to Mrs. Maria Pain, daughter of George and Jane Humphreys; she was born July 10th, 1830. The fruits of their marriage is a family of four children, one of whom is now deceased. Mr. Dean is at present residing on his farm in Littleton township, enjoying good health.

Details from this short biography share important information about this Irish gentleman, information I might not otherwise find. Were he my ancestor, before I headed for Ireland, I would have a much more focused area in which to look — County Dennygaul (knowing the counties in Ireland and the Irish brogue as I do, I am sure this refers to County Donegal – on the northwest coast of Ireland) — as opposed to trying to scour the whole of Ireland in search of information about William Dean. Also, the details of his arrival date, age at arrival and subsequent movements within America give me clues to uncovering other documents – immigration and naturalization records, censuses, etc., that will help me further refine my search for William Dean and his ancestors.

Military Records

A special note about military records as they relate to the Irish. I cover military records extensively in several other genealogy books (*Quillen's Essentials of Genealogy*: *Mastering Census and Military Records* and *Troubleshooter's Guide*). When they came to the US, many of the Irish became fierce patriots, and threads of their lives can be picked up in military records. Especially for those Irish who made their way to America in the post-Potato Famine years, they and their sons chose to fight for the new nation they called home.

Even before the Civil War, the Irish made an appreciable impact on the establishment of America. One of my favorite quotes about American history and the Irish is by Lord Mountjoy. Addressing the English Parliament after the Revolutionary War, he said:

We have lost America through the Irish!

That was not an idle statement, and probably not even an overstatement. At the time of the Revolutionary War, one in eight American colonists were Irish. Of the fifty-six signers of the Declaration of Independence, nine were born in Ireland. It has been estimated that between one third and one half of the Continental Army was Irish. So when Lord Mountjoy said Britain had lost America through the Irish, he was not exaggerating.

If you're lucky enough to be Irish…well, you're lucky enough!

And the Civil War was a place where the Irish distinguished themselves as American citizens, and again helped to shape our national history. The Irish joined in droves. Some to fight for their country. Some to gain citizenship quickly (honorably discharged Union soldiers could earn citizenship after one year's service, rather than waiting five years). Some doubtless joined and fought for the bounty – as high as $700 in some cases (roughly equivalent to $14,000 in today's dollars). That represented about a decade's worth of earnings in Ireland at that time.

Regardless of the reason, over 170,000 Irish men fought in the Union Army (about one in twelve Union soldiers) and over 40,000 fought on the Confederate side. The Union Army had twenty-six generals who were born in Ireland, and the Confederates had five. (By contrast, the Confederates had one British general, and the Union had two British generals, along with one lone Scotsman!)

So if your Irish ancestor was the age to have served during any of the wars of the United States, military records may well provide information that will help you know where to look in Ireland for their family members.

Returning to Fred, he was a post-Civil War immigrant – born in 1891 and immigrating to America in 1915. I checked various websites to see if I could locate him in the World War I draft registration card database, but no luck. I sort of expected that, as I note from his Petition for Citizenship he was in the military from 1917 to 1919. It is unclear to me whether he would have served in the United States or the British army or navy. He came to America in 1915, but given the fact that he was not yet an American citizen, I suspect his service was with Britain. More records to check out!

I also thought it wise to check the World War II draft registration cards to see if Fred had completed that registration. This registration was taken in April 1942. It was for men who were born between April 28, 1877 and February 16, 1897. The government was not seeking to draft these older men (ages 45 to 64), but instead was gleaning information on the industrial skills and capacity of the workforce. They wouldn't be used for military service, but the information provided the government with an inventory of the manpower resources available at that time. Apparently the resources weren't sufficient to meet our war-time manufacturing needs – remember Rosie the Riveter? Over 10,000,000 men completed these draft registration cards, and they are available, many of them online.

Checking for Fred, I was successful in finding him – I think – at FamilySearch.org. He had completed a World War II draft registration card. Here's the information I found for him:

Name: Frederick John McQuillan
Residence: 107 East 126th Street, New York City, NY
Age: 49
Birth date: July 22, 1893
Birth place: County Down, Ireland
Name of person who will always know your address: Mrs. John Hanratty,
    325 East 33rd Street, New York City, NY

Okay – so at first glance, it appears this is the same Frederick John McQuillan. Note that Mrs. John Hanratty is the person Fred indicated would always know his address – another tie to Margaret Hanratty, who is, by the way, living in the same place she has been living in 1920.

But now I run into a bit of a conundrum. The data on the WW II draft registration card conflicts with information Fred provided elsewhere on other documents. Following is a chart of the birth date and place information I have for Frederick John McQuillan:

Source	Birth Date	Birth place
1920 census	age 28 in 1920; (1891 or 1892)	Ireland
1930 Census	age 36 (1893 or 1894)	Irish Free State
Petition for Citizenship	August 25, 1891	Dundalk, Ireland
Passenger List	23 on August 25, 1915 (1892)	Dundalk, Ireland
WWII Draft Registration	July 22, 1893	Co. Down, Ireland

What to do, what to do? While it is possible there are two men named Frederick John McQuillan, it is less possible that Margaret Hanratty would know both of them well enough to vouch for them as a witness on government documents. Still – it *is* possible – they could be cousins, both named after a revered ancestor.

However, the Petition for Citizenship and WW II draft registration card were both signed by Fred, and I compared the signatures on the documents. While I am not a handwriting expert, it was pretty clear that the same person signed both documents, so I am reasonably certain that even though several critical elements (date and place of birth) are different, we are looking at records for the same person.

Signature from his Petition for Citizenship

Signature from WW II draft registration card

There are other sets of military records that are worth searching to see if you can glean information about your Irish ancestors. For example:

- Revolutionary War pension records – while not as information-laden, pension applications from the Revolutionary War may also contain genealogical information. Remember – it has been estimated that between one third and one half of the soldiers in the Continental army were Irish. I found the pension application for my fifth great grandfather and learned such things as:
  - His residence at the time of application
  - Birth date and place
  - The fact he was married

- Civil War pension records – these records often grant researchers rich rewards for their effort. I have found vital genealogical information about service men ancestors of mine as well as their spouses and children: name, date and place of birth, wife's maiden name, names and birth dates of all children under age 16, marriage date, and even the names of children and the dates they died. As mentioned earlier, over 210,000 Irish men fought in the US Civil War, and they left an abundance of records behind them.

- World War I draft registration cards – like their younger cousins, World War I draft registration cards may provide information that will help you unlock your ancestor's past. All men – US citizens or not — ages 18 to 45 who were residing in the United States during the World War I years were required to complete draft registration cards. Estimates are that 98% of men complied with this requirement. These cards provided much the same information as are found on draft registration cards for the next war: name, age, address, birth date and place, the name of someone who would always know where they were, nearest relative, immigration status, etc.

So don't overlook military records as sources of information that might provide a clue for finding that elusive Irish ancestor of yours. You can get a more thorough treatment of this important set of records in *Quillen's Essentials of Genealogy: Mastering Census and Military Records* and *Troubleshooter's Guide.*

> Don't overlook military records as sources of information on my ancestors!

US Records Summary

Thank you for your patience in hanging with me in searching for Irish roots by beginning here in the US. Hopefully I have convinced you that overlooking US records when searching for your Irish ancestors may make your job unnecessarily difficult. Following is the information I have been able to glean on this shirt-tail Irish cousin of mine from US records:

Name: Frederick John McQuillan

Birth date: August 25, 1891 (two sources) or July 22, 1893 (one source)

Birth place: Dundalk, Ireland (three sources) or County Down, Ireland (one source)

Immigrated to US: 1915 (two sources) or 1914 (one source)

Naturalized: 1927

Wife's name: Catherine McQuillan

Wife's birth date: December 18, 1899

Wife's birthplace: Ireland

Children's names and birth dates:

    Patrick, April 15, 1921, born Ireland

    Margaret, May 23, 1923, born Ireland

Father: Felix McQuillan

Niece: Jane Lynch

Residence: Crossmaglen, County Armagh, Ireland

BIG MAC OR BIG MC?

From time to time I will read a genealogy blurb that says names beginning with "Mc" are Irish, while those beginning with "Mac" are Scottish. In his book *The Surnames of Ireland*, Edward MacLysaght indicates this is essentially rubbish. He contends that "Mc" is merely an abbreviation for "Mac."

While I believe Mr. MacLysaght, I have to admit I have reason to wonder. While traveling in Scotland a few years ago, I opened a telephone directory. There were pages and pages (and pages) of Macs, yet only a relatively few Mcs. Conversely, on the same trip, I was in Ireland and opened a telephone directory, and found pages and pages (and pages) of Mcs, but only a relatively few Macs. Coincidence, I am sure, but still, it gives one pause.

As you can see, the information for Frederick John McQuillan is rounding nicely into shape. Now, I can head overseas to see if I can't find more information about this cousin of mine. Using the above information, I can focus my search around several key genealogical elements.

Records in Ireland

Okay – now you've arrived at the point where you can begin searching for your ancestors by going to Irish records. To this point, we have dealt almost exclusively with records gleaned by the United States government, but now we'll move to the Emerald Isle itself. Some of the records we'll explore are still available online, but many of them are available only via a visit to Ireland or Northern Ireland.

That last is an important distinction. There is a difference between Ireland and Northern Ireland that is more than just geographical relativity. Northern Ireland is a part of the United Kingdom of Great Britain – and Ireland is not (they were for about 700 years, but that is no longer the case).

I have mentioned that I made contact with and have visited a number of distant cousins in Northern Ireland. On one of my many visits with them, it occurred to me to ask them, "Do you consider yourself British or Irish?" I was surprised by their answer: "Why, British, of course." I suppose

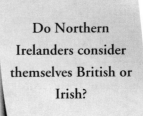

Do Northern Irelanders consider themselves British or Irish?

I had just assumed since they were on the island of Ireland, they considered themselves Irish. Not so. Since that time, I have read many articles, reviewed many studies, etc., and it appears that most citizens of Northern Ireland consider themselves British.

However, for the purposes of this book, we will consider and address Northern Ireland's genealogical records in the Irish section of this book. I hope that isn't too upsetting to my Northern Ireland cousins!

Before we begin opening up those Irish records, let's talk about some important geographical information that you'll likely need in your research of Irish records.

Irish Geographic Units

I once met the unofficial county genealogist of County Antrim, Ireland. My friend and fellow genealogist, Felix, claims with all humility that he is not the county genealogist, officially or unofficially. However, he has in fact spent (and continues to spend) a great deal of time researching the key families of County Antrim. Several years ago, I purchased a book Felix had written about the families of County Antrim: *Townlands, Peoples and Traditions* (Felix McKillop, 2006, County Antrim, Northern Ireland).

The main reason I mention Felix's book is because it introduced me to an important genealogical term with which most Americans are unfamiliar:

townlands. It turns out a townland is a subdivision smaller than a parish, which is smaller than a province. Following is a little more about townlands and other geographic subdivisions. Not knowing about one or more of them may cause you to run screaming into the night as you strive to make sense out of Irish records you find.

- **Townland** – this is an area I suspect you may not be familiar with. It is roughly equivalent to the township in American vernacular, but is generally much smaller. A townland may be as small as one acre (!) to several thousand acres. It could be a small town. As you look at older Irish records, you may well run into this term. Estimates place the number of townlands in Ireland at around 64,000! They are the smallest geographical units you will run into in your genealogical research. Townlands are gathered together into a civil parish (not to be confused with a Catholic Church parish).
- **Parish** — a series of townlands together make up a parish. The parishes referred to here are generally equivalent to the parishes of the Church of Ireland, the predominant (state) church extant in Ireland during the Middle Ages. These parishes are generally much smaller than Catholic parishes, and again, should not be mistaken for Catholic parishes.
- **Poor Law Union** – also known as a PLU, this is a term you have probably not heard, but if you do much work with Irish records, you are sure to run into them. PLUs were jurisdictional areas that typically consisted of a number of parishes, and were considered civil registration districts. Older records in particular will contain the name of a PLU, rather than a parish or county name. Some of the PLUs in the country carry the names of Irish towns, lakes, etc. (or is it the other way around?!). A typical PLU may consist of from twenty to forty parishes, and a county may be made up of from two to fifteen PLUs (most common is four or five). PLUs grew out of the workhouse system – a sort of unemployment assistance effort for areas that were particularly poor or struggling

financially. If you go to *www.seanruad.com,* you can find what PLU your townland or parish was part of. Use this if you find a record that has a PLU on it.

Further to townlands, while I was writing this book, I reached out to my friend Felix McKillop in Northern Ireland to get a local take on townlands. Here are his thoughts:

> Townlands are unique to Ireland and are crucial for genealogists in studying family roots. Virtually all Irish records for the 19th century and earlier, as well as most of the 20th century, deal with townlands. Parish records are important for baptisms, marriages and deaths and sometimes refer to townlands — where they do they make genealogists' work so much easier. Landed estate records often give lists of names of tenants within townlands but only name "head of family" as they are simply used as means of registering and collecting rents.

By the way, if your ancestors hail from County Antrim, on the northern coast of Northern Ireland, you may want to touch bases with Felix and pick up his book I mentioned above: *Townlands, Peoples and Traditions.* You can order a copy from Felix at *fmckillop@lineone.net.* Unfortunately, he's not interested in doing research in County Antrim for you, even at a price — I asked!

Townlands are important Irish geographical units for genealogists.

Irish Censuses

Irish censuses were kept beginning in 1801, but the 1821, 1831, 1841 and 1851 censuses were almost entirely destroyed in 1922. The 1901 and 1911 censuses are available to the public. Additional censuses were taken in 1926,

1936, 1946, 1951, 1961, 1966, 1971 1981 and 1991, but those won't be open to the public for some time to come, since like the British censuses, they won't be released until 100 years have passed.

Speaking of the 1901 and 1911 censuses, let's revisit Frederick John McQuillan. As a refresher, we identified the following information for Frederick from US records:

Name: Frederick John McQuillan
Birth date: August 25, 1891 (two sources) or July 22, 1893 (one source)
Birth place: Dundalk, Ireland (three sources) or County Down, Ireland (one source)
Immigrated to US: 1915 (two sources) or 1914 (one source)
Naturalized: 1927
Wife's name: Catherine McQuillan
Wife's birth date: December 18, 1899
Wife's birthplace: Ireland
Children's names and birth dates:
 Patrick, April 15, 1921, born Ireland
 Margaret, May 23, 1923, born Ireland
Father: Felix McQuillan
Niece: Jane Lynch
Residence: Crossmaglen, County Armagh, Ireland

So, from that information gleaned from US records, I know that he was born in either Dundalk or County Down sometime between 1891 and 1893. So, let's see if we can find a family in the 1901 census with a nine- or ten-year-old son named Frederick John (or Fred, Freddie, John, Johnny, etc.) living in Dundalk, County Louth, Ireland, or in County Down, Ireland. (Remember your history – Northern Ireland didn't come into existence until the treaty with Britain in 1921.)

There are a number of websites I could use to access the 1901 Irish Census. The one I chose to use was *www.census.nationalarchives.ie*. I decide to start with Dundalk, since three of the sources cited that as where Fred was born. I get to the *Search* box, select *1901 census* and enter McQuillan in the *Surname* box and Fred in the *Forename* (first name) box. I also enter County Louth to narrow the search, and click *Search*, and…nothing. Hmmm, not what I was hoping. I try Frederick and get…nothing. Some websites allow wildcards, so I try *Fred** in the *Forename* box and I have some success! Here's what I get:

Surname	Forename	Address	City	Age	Sex
McQuillan,	Freddie	Mary Street	Dundalk	9	M

Okay – so I am a little excited. I know the 1901 census was taken in April 1901, and know that Fred was born in either July or August, so he would have been 9 years old in April 1901. I decide to look at the rest of the family, and this is what I find (see table on next page):

While I am not quite ready to declare victory and move on, this is promising information. Especially since neither Fred or Felix are common names, but the fact that a lot of the information in US records points to a birth place of Dundalk in or about 1891 leads me to believe I may have found Frederick John's family. I decided to check the 1911 census also, and here's what I found (see table on page 53):

The 1911 record also shows that Frederick is a boiler maker in the ship yards. You may recall that in the 1920 US census he listed his occupation as an ironworker in a shipyard, and in his Petition for Citizenship he listed his occupation as a riveter. All these similar occupations could again add credence to my feeling that this is the same Frederick.

Surname	Forename	Age	Sex	Relation to Head	Religion
McQuillan	Felix	37	M	Head of Family	Catholic
McQuillan	Bridget	38	F	Wife	Catholic
McQuillan	Mary	19	F	Daughter	Catholic
McQuillan	James	18	M	Son	Catholic
McQuillan	Emlyn	14	F	Daughter	Catholic
McQuillan	Lizzie	11	F	Daughter	Catholic
McQuillan	Freddie	9	M	Son	Catholic
McQuillan	Robert	5	M	Son	Catholic
McQuillan	Peter	3	M	Son	Catholic

Surname	Forename	Age	Sex	Relation to Head	Religion	Birthplace
McQuillan	Felix	46	M	Head of Family	Catholic	Armagh
McQuillan	Bridget	47	F	Wife	Catholic	Louth
McQuillan	Mary	25	F	Daughter	Catholic	Louth
McQuillan	James	24	M	Son	Catholic	Louth
McQuillan	Evelyn	22	F	Daughter	Catholic	Louth
McQuillan	Elizabeth	20	F	Daughter	Catholic	Louth
McQuillan	Frederick	18	M	Son	Catholic	Louth
McQuillan	Robert	16	M	Son	Catholic	Louth
McQuillan	Peter	14	M	Son	Catholic	Louth

You may recall I was thinking Mary Hanratty, with whom Frederick boarded in 1920, and who kept showing up on government documents – like his Petition for Citizenship and his World War II draft registration card – might have been his sister. As I looked at the 1901 census, I thought, "Maybe Mary is really Mary Margaret in Dundalk, and is also Margaret Hanratty in New York." Alas – good thought, but that's not to be. The 1911 census indicated Bridget was the mother of 9 children, 7 of whom were alive. But it also listed seven children living with her in 1911. And if you'll recall, Mary Hanratty said she had immigrated to the US in 1905. So, while it's possible she moved back to Ireland with her family, and then moved to New York in time to be enumerated in the 1920 census, it's not probable. But I would really suspect she is related to that family somehow, so I'll keep her name and information handy.

Another item that is worth noting. Recall that on his passenger record, Frederick said he was going to visit his niece, Jane Lynch. That could be her married name, but if it is her maiden name, perhaps she is Frederick's mother's sister, so his mother's maiden name may be Lynch. As I look for marriage records, I'll be looking for that as a possibility.

I decided – for the sake of this book and my readers – to Google Felix McQuillan and Bridget. I did so, and found a Genealogy.com message board with the following message:

> Hello there, I am a descendant of the McQuillans, Dundalk, Co. Louth. My mother's mother was Elizabeth McQuillan born 26-5-1889. Her mother and father were, Bridget Kearney and Felix McQuillan of Williamsons Place, Dundalk. They were married 11-1-1882. There are two sides to the McQuillans in Dundalk. The Co Louth line of McQuillans has a history in Crossmaglen, 3 miles to the west of Louth. They had a lace making factory in

Crossmaglen and were quite prominent in the 19th century also as butchers.

I hope this info is of some help in your research.

Good Luck!

Patricia

Checking that information against what I learned in the 1911 census, it appears I may now have the maiden name of Frederick John McQuillan's mother – she was Bridget Kearney, according to Patricia from the message board post. (So much for my hypothesis that Lynch might have been her maiden name! Oh well – you win some, you lose some!) The 1911 census also said that Bridget and Felix had been married 27 years, which makes their marriage about 1884, which is close to Patricia's claim that her great grandparents were married in 1882. It would be good for me to reach out to Patricia to see if she can provide me with her source for the marriage date for Felix and Bridget.

Note also that the genealogy message board message shows Elizabeth as having been born in December 1889. The 1901 census lists Lizzie (diminutive for Elizabeth) as 11 years old in April 1901 – which would be correct. Note also that Patricia says the Louth McQuillans (Fred's family) had a lace-making factory in Crossmaglen. Recall that several of the passenger lists on which we found Fred showed Crossmaglen as his residence before departing for America.

I decided to go to Ancestry.com (international version) and see if I could find anything about Felix McQuillan and Bridget Kearney McQuillan. As I was poking around, I was able to locate a photograph of the headstone for

Felix and Bridget, along with a young grandson who shared their burial plot. The tombstone is in the Dowdallshill Cemetery, Dundalk, Ireland, and the transcription reads:

> Erected by Felix McQuillan
>
> In Loving Memory of his wife Bridget
>
> Who died 30th April 1935
>
> Also Daniel McQuillan,
>
> Her grandson, died 3rd December 1937
>
> And the above
>
> Felix McQuillan
>
> Died 19th January 1944

I was able to locate all this information in a relatively short amount of time, all because I had done research in US records before trying to jump over to Irish records. Not to have done the research I could here with US records, would have made my search for Fred much like seeking a needle in a haystack.

Remember – search US records first for clues to Irish records.

The moral of this genealogical story – search those US records first!

Civil Registration

Civil registration (the registering of births, marriages and death by the government) began in Ireland in 1864 — much later than most other western European countries. Non-Catholic civil registration commenced in 1845.

In 1922 a nasty civil war erupted in Ireland over differences between the treaty with England that gave most of Ireland her freedom, but left six northern counties of Ulster as part of England – the area on the Emerald Isle now known as Northern Ireland. The genealogical significance of this civil war is that during the fighting, approximately 900 years of Irish records were destroyed when one of the groups booby-trapped the Four Courts, a government building where those genealogy records were stored. The booby-trap was tripped, and although no soldiers were killed, nearly a thousand years of Irish genealogical records went up in smoke.

Since that time, the National Archives has been busy trying to cobble together records from other sources that were not destroyed – land records spread across the country, wills and probate records, etc.

However – all is not lost. Many civil registration records were kept within the Poor Law Union areas of the country. Many of those records have been extracted by the LDS Church (and available through their genealogy website *FamilySearch.org)* and can be found in their databases, although most of the available information are abstracts and/or indexes as opposed to images of the actual records.

In addition, copies of birth, marriage and death certificates can be gotten from the *General Register Office* in Roscommon Ireland for the Republic. Send your request to:

> General Register Office
> Government Offices
> Convent Road
> Roscommon, Ireland

For specific information you can visit their website at *www.groireland.ie.*

They are quick to point out they do not do genealogical research for you, but will either provide certified copies or photocopies of the birth, marriage or death registers.

And for the North, you have a friend for your genealogical research in the Public Record Office of Northern Ireland (PRONI). Much of the information available there can be gotten online at the following website: *www.nidirect.gov.uk/index/do-it-online/leisure-home-and-community-online/ research-your-family-and-local-history.htm*. Fees are associated with requests and research, and the website does a pretty good job of identifying the costs of each type request you may have.

They have done extensive work digitizing many of Northern Ireland's archival records. Their holdings include:

- **The Ulster Covenant** – On September 28, 1912, nearly half a million men and women of Ulster (the northern-most counties on the Emerald Isle) signed the Ulster Covenant. The Ulster Covenant was a formal protest against the Home Rule Bill which had been recently introduced to the English Parliament, calling for the separation of Ireland from England and allowing Ireland autonomous rule. As you might suspect, signatories were generally Protestant, so if your ancestor's name appeared there, you may not find them in Catholic Church records (that's not an absolute, but generally it was the Protestants who opposed Home Rule). Nearly half a million signatures is significant, when you consider Northern Ireland is about the same size as Connecticut!
- **Freeholder's Lists** – These are lists of people who had the opportunity to vote (or voted) at elections. During much of the 18th century (1727 to 1793), Catholics were disenfranchised, and only Protestants could vote. Not only was voting limited to Protestants, they also had to own a freehold worth 40 shillings to be allowed to vote. In 1793, the law was

changed, and Catholics were also allowed to vote if they owned land and buildings worth at least 40 shillings. So again – if your ancestor's name shows up on a freehold list between 1727 and 1793, they were Protestant, not Catholic. The freeholder lists comprise approximately 5,500 sheets of pre-1840s voters' registers and poll lists. The collection has been indexed, so finding individuals' names is much easier than poring over 5,500 records. The records are divided into two categories:

Registers — details of those who had registered to vote

Poll Books — lists of voters and the candidates for whom they voted

• **Street Directories** – PRONI has digitized and made available the Ulster street directories between 1819 and 1900. These are like telephone directories – but without the telephone numbers! This is an excellent source to use to locate families in what eventually became Northern Ireland.

PRONI is a great friend to genealogists doing research on their families in Northern Ireland. In addition to the online records cited above, they have extensive holdings of microfilm and physical documents. Unfortunately, these records, at the date of this writing, are only available through a visit to their offices. Their offices are located at:

Public Record Office of Northern Ireland
2 Titanic Boulevard
Belfast, Northern Ireland
pronie@dcalni.gov.uk
Tel. 44-028-90 534800

If you are planning a visit to review records, you may want to call or e-mail ahead of time to make sure the records you are seeking are available. If, for example, you are hoping to search the Church of Ireland parish records for

Armagh, make sure they are in their holdings and available for viewing. An excellent review of records available at PRONI is available at *www.proni.gov.uk/index/research_and_records_held/catalogues_guides_indexes _and_leaflets/information_leaflets.htm*. Detailed information on the following sets of records is available there:

- Ulster Censuses
- Wills
- Street Directories
- Griffiths valuation
- Gravestone inscriptions
- Tithe applotment records
- Burial records
- Pedigrees and genealogical collection

That last item may be of interest if you are researching your ancestors in Ulster. PRONI holds several extensive pedigree and genealogical papers. One is an extract of wills from all over Ireland, covering the period between 1536 and 1800.

Wills and probate records

Wills in Ireland, like wills in any society, provide interesting and informative input for genealogical researchers. Generally speaking, the wills you will find in Ireland will be for the landed gentry, but occasionally you can find wills for the "unwashed masses." Typically, you'll find most of the following information in wills:

- Name of the testator
- Beneficiaries, which may include any members of his family
- Witnesses (pay attention to these – they may be family members)

- Name(s) of the executor(s) (could be a member of the family – often an eldest son)
- Address of the testator
- Date the will was made
- Date the will was probated

As you can see, this information may shed a great deal of light on a family at a certain point of time. It can identify spouse and children, perhaps even grandchildren, nieces and nephews and others.

Personally, I like to research wills because they may also paint a picture of the family, their lives and the things they placed value on at the time. They help enrich my understanding of these ancestors of mine.

Alas, as we have detailed earlier in this chapter, many records were lost in 1922 during the Irish Civil War. Many of those records were wills. However, the good news is that copies (or originals) of many of those wills were also stored across the nation in various locations. A good starting point to try and find wills will be one of the various Heritage Centers in Ireland (see **Appendix A**). Also, you may find wills and probate records in both the National Archives and General Register Office in the Republic of Ireland as well as the Public Records Office of Northern Ireland. Websites for these entities indicate wills are available to view in their respective reading rooms.

> Irish wills and probate records are excellent sources of genealogical information.

Parish Records

Most European countries with heavy Catholic populations (Ireland is 84% Catholic and Northern Ireland is 40% Catholic), owe a great debt to the Catholic Church for their prolific record keeping. In most countries, their church records (birth, marriage, death, baptism, confirmation, etc.) began in at least the mid-1500s as a result of the Council of Trent. In many cases, parish priests began keeping those sorts of records long before the decree required it. Catholic churches in Ireland were no different. So that makes genealogical research in Ireland simple, right? Just contact the local Catholic parish where your ancestors lived and – ta da! – tons of information.

That would probably be so, except for the fact that in the three centuries between the Council of Trent and the early 1800s, the British government was especially nasty toward the Catholics in general, and the Catholic Church in particular. Unfortunately, that meant one of the activities that went by the wayside was the keeping of records. Parish records for most of the parishes in Ireland begin in the early to mid-1800s. Civil registration wasn't required in Ireland until 1864, and the vast majority of records prior to that are parish records. A couple of parishes (Waterford, Wexford and Galway) have a smattering of records that extend back to the late 1600s. Other than that, few parishes in Ireland have records that date earlier than the beginning of the 19th century.

When I say parish records, I am referring primarily to baptism, marriage and death / burial records. If you are able to locate these records, they are great genealogical finds. Sometimes, some of the Catholic priests really got into their record-keeping responsibilities, and provided a little enhanced information about the individuals. Consider some of the additional information provided by the Catholic parish priest in Inch, Ireland for deaths that occurred in his parish between 1788 and 1872 (see table on next page):

As you can see, sometimes Church death records go beyond just telling us a little about the deceased. Several other entries from this Catholic Church in Inch contained remarks that the individual had been one of the early settlers in the parish, or that there were once many of the same surname in

Surname	First name	Death Date	Remarks
Gibson	William	24 December, 1788	of Ballygalley
Graham	William	24 December, 1788	of Annacloy, father of Ann (wife of William Rea) of the Rann
Rea	William	21 June 1792	of The Rann, Grandfather of Edward; Edward Rea married Ann Thompson and was father of John, James and Edward Rea
Maxwell	Edward	25 January, 1793	son of John Waring Maxwell and husband of Dorothy of Finnebrogue
Kirkwood	Thomas	15 January, 1794	Quaker and Scottish stock – now extinct

the parish but they were all gone with the death of this individual, etc. And how do you find similar Irish parish records? My first suggestion is for you to see if they are online. The records listed above from Inch, Ireland were online and available with a few key strokes and a click or two of the mouse. (The Inch parish records were found at *ancestorsatrest.com/church_records/ inch_parish_records_burials.shtml*.)

Ancestry.com has a number of nice collections of parish and civil records from Ireland, including some of the following collections:

• Ireland Births and Baptisms, 1620-1911
• Ireland Catholic parish baptisms, 1742 – 1881
• Irish records extraction database, 1600 — 1864

Baptismal records are a good source of genealogical information. Generally speaking, the information contained in baptismal records includes:

• Name of child
• Date of baptism
• Father's name
• Mother's maiden name

Often, the names of godparents were also included. These are important names to keep handy – they were often an aunt or uncle of the child – their mother's brother or sister, or their father's brother or sister.

Baptismal records generally included the child's name as well as his parents' names

Catholic marriage records contain about what you would expect:
• Name of groom
• Maiden name of bride
• Marriage date

Generally, names of witnesses were listed and again, it's important to keep these names, as they may be relatives. Occasionally, the parents of the bride and groom are listed. I have seen marriage entries that included the residences of all parties (groom, bride, witnesses and parents). Sometimes (although not the rule), marriage registers included the relationship (if any) of the witnesses to the married parties. Some marriage records include the ages of the bride and groom, as well as the groom's occupation.

Death is an important and inevitable part of life, and death records kept by the Catholic Church again provide good information. In a bit of a records anomaly, as good as those hard-working Catholic priests were through the years, about half the parishes in Ireland did not keep death or burial records. And even those who kept those records were sometimes sporadic. When they did keep them, typically, their records include:

• Name of the deceased
• Death date
• Occasionally some comment about the individual (wife of _____, husband of _____, father of _____, _____, and _____).

I can tell I have convinced you of the value of these Catholic Church parish records, so now let's talk about a few places where you can find them.

1. **National Library of Ireland**, Kildare Street, Dublin 2, Ireland, *www.nli.ie/ en/family-history-introduction.aspx*. The e-mail address for their family history section is *genealogy@nli.ie*. This is the national depository of many of Ireland's records on microfilm. It specializes in Catholic parish registers. The office is open to the public, and you can go here and pore over microfilmed records to your heart's content. Before you go, write to or e-mail them to determine what records they have available for the parish or diocese where your family lived – include all the information you are

looking for. The National Library undertook to microfilm the Catholic Church's parish records back in the 1950s and 1960s. They were successful in microfilming a little over 90% of the parish records. That's the good news. The bad news is…none of those are online. If we could convince them to put their records online, it would be a good thing. But, until that happens, your only choice if you want to view those records is to visit Ireland (so it's not all bad!).

Here's a short blurb from the library's family history section on their website:

> The Library holds microfilm copies of the records of most Roman Catholic parishes in Ireland for the years up to 1880 and in some cases to 1900. For further information on these registers, please read our Family History information leaflet entitled *Parish Registers in the National Library of Ireland* (which can be downloaded from their website).

The library also has land valuation records and tithe applotment records available for review. These records were compiled between 1823 and 1838 as a survey of titheable land in each parish. (They do not cover cities or towns). In general, the information contained in the Tithe Books is as follows:

Don't forget about townlands!

- name of occupier
- name of townland (remember the discussion earlier in this chapter about townlands…?)
- acreage
- classification of land
- amount of tithe due.

The Land Valuation records at the National Library are a record of the land and who lived on it between 1848 and 1864. Since many of Ireland's 19th-century genealogy records were destroyed, these records are a valuable substitute and provide at least some information to researchers.

2. Local Heritage Centers – above I mentioned the National Library of Ireland had microfilmed the majority of the parish records of Ireland. However, around the country, local Heritage Centers (Antrim Heritage Centre, Clare Heritage Centre, Ulster Historical Foundation, etc.) have done some work to put some of these parish records online. **Appendix A** has a listing of Heritage Centres in Ireland, with information about them – e-mail addresses, websites, and whether or not there is a cost to view their records. Many organizations in Ireland allow you to view their records for a price – typically you purchase credits, and then each record viewed costs so many credits (I hope that pricing scheme doesn't catch on here in the US!). (Thanks to Dennis A. Hogan for doing all the legwork to put the list together, and for allowing me to provide it to you in this book.)

3. The Church of Jesus Christ of Latter-day Saints (LDS Church) is a prolific genealogy organization. As of this writing, they have microfilmed about a third of the parish records in Ireland, and those microfilms are available through their Family History Center (FHC) network. The microfilms are held at the LDS Church's Family History Library in Salt Lake City, Utah. You can visit them there, or you can order microfilms to be sent to a local FHC near you. There are over 4,500 FHCs throughout the world at last count. You do not have to be a member of the LDS Church to enjoy this service. In fact, in a majority of the FHCs, they are visited more by non-LDS genealogists than by members of the LDS Church.

Ordering microfilms is easy and inexpensive – a few bucks for the postage – and the microfilms stay at the local FHC for you to view over a six-week period. Sometimes, the LDS Church will send the microfilms for you to view at a State Library location. Call ahead to your local State Library to make sure they participate in this network.

Chancery Records

Often in my books, I encourage my readers with the fact that new records are coming online seemingly daily, and if you can't find something online today, just keep checking every now and then.

A great example of that occurred to me recently. I have been working with Irish records for years, and while I was writing this book, I ran across a notice that a new records source had just become available – chancery letters.

As you know from earlier in this chapter, an epic tragedy destroyed nearly a thousand years of Irish records when the records hall of the Four Courts was destroyed during Ireland's Civil War. However, in a labor of scholarly love and scholastic excellence, a group of men and women worked for four decades to recreate over 20,000 medieval records.

How do you recreate records? Well, in this case, many of the records that were destroyed were chancery rolls – rolls of paper where information was entered from original documents. In some cases, those original documents were also destroyed, but in many instances, those original documents were kept in various places – in county archives, in English archives (remember – England occupied and ruled Ireland for over 700 years), and in other places.

Scholars from Dublin's Trinity College rolled up their sleeves and built a database of all those documents. They are available today at *CIRCLE: A Calendar of Irish Chancery Letters, c.1244–1509.* It can be accessed at *chancery.tcd.ie/.* Many of the documents are not genealogical – individuals petitioning the English throne for a favor or to seek redress for some situation, or to request pardon from a fine (*lots* of those)!

Notwithstanding the governmental nature of most of the documents, many have genealogical information mixed in. Consider, for example, this interesting plea sent to King Edward III from Comare McComarre on 7 May 1374 — 650 years ago! (I have retained the original spelling, punctuation and abbreviations):

> To the T. and chamberlains of the Ex.
>
> Comare McComarre, chieftain of his lineage, has shown by petition before the governor and keeper of Ire., and others of the council, that O Breen of Thomond, the K.'s Irish enemy and rebel, lately waged war on **John McComarre, father of Comare,** now dcd, and wasted the greater part the lands and tenements of the said John in co. Limerick and adjacent part because John and his men became the K.'s faithful lieges. After the death of his father, Comare gathered a great retinue of defensible men to the number of four hundred to fight the said Obreen, whom he retained at his own expense from Christmas until now, whereby the faithful people of those parts were much comforted and better able to restrain the malice of Obreen. Comare can no longer maintain his men or oppose Obreen in the future without suitable aid from the K. and he has therefore sought remedy. Because James Butler, e. Ormond, the mayor and bailiffs of Limerick, and other faithful subjects of the K. in those parts have testified before the council as to the truth of the premises, and the said town and environs are threatened by Obreen unless Comare repulses him, the K. by advice of council granted Comare 50m for the said arrears, as a gift. ORDER to pay Comare those 50m, receiving from him letters of acquittance.

Attested: William Windsor, governor and keeper of Ire.
Authorized: By petition of council.

> Chancery records are often overlooked, but can provide excellent information.

Besides being intensely interesting to me, it also listed Comare's father's name: John McComarre. It allowed me to make a linkage between a father and a son who lived over 650 years ago.

A Bold Idea

I shared the following information in *Secrets of Tracing Your Ancestors*, but I am going to share it here as well. Not only did this occasion some wonderful experiences for my family and me, but I have heard from a number of my readers that they did the same thing and enjoyed similar results. Therefore, I want to share it again with those of you who are reading this book.

Five of my eight great grandparents' surnames are Irish, so I have a special fondness for the Emerald Isle in my heart. Before my first trip there, I decided to try and contact some long-lost cousins. Never shy, I decided on a bold plan. First of all, it required a letter written to my Irish cousins. This is what I wrote:

Dear McQuillan Family,

Greetings from your long-lost American cousin! Doubtless you were unaware that you had a long-lost American cousin, at least not this one. But you do. In 1635 my tenth-great grandfather Teague McQuillan left County Antrim to see if he could improve his fortunes in the wilds of America. Ten generations later here I am, intensely interested in visiting the part of Ireland he left so long ago.

But that's not all. I am as interested in meeting other members of the McQuillan family as I am in seeing the Emerald Isle. Hence my letter. In May of next year, my wife and I are planning to visit Ireland and would like to be able to visit some of the cousins as well as the part of Ireland Teague was from. We will be in Northern Ireland from May 3 through May 10, and would love to stop by and meet you. Please let me know if you will be available during that time, and we'll arrange our schedule to meet with you.

I know this may seem rather presumptuous and just a bit bold, but I really am interested in meeting other members of the McQuillan Clan, however distant along the family tree they may be. Thanks, and I look forward to meeting with you when we are there.

– Daniel Quillen

After I typed the letter, I made and signed twenty copies. Then, from a map of Northern Ireland, I selected twenty small towns in County Antrim, where my Irish ancestors were from. (I think something like this will work better with small towns rather than larger cities.) I addressed each envelope with the family name and the name of one of the towns. For example, one of the letters was addressed as follows:

McQuillan Family
Larne
Northern Ireland

And then, in the bottom left-hand corner of the front of the envelope I wrote: *POSTMASTER: PLEASE DELIVER THIS LETTER TO ANY McQUILLAN FAMILY IN THE VICINITY.*

I sent the letters six months prior to our trip to Ireland. I was delighted to receive seven responses to my rather unorthodox method of contacting family. But the results were marvelous! We met a number of these Irish families, were entertained in their homes, and they showed us great kindness. We left much richer for our time with them.

I sent those letters over fifteen years ago, and I still visit those cousins every year or two, and we often stay in their homes, go to dinner, etc.

As a special bonus, they provided us with a wonderful genealogical treasure. Literally hundreds of names were provided to us, members of the family that I had not previously known about. They took us to the "old homestead," prowled through graveyards with us helping us locate the gravestones of past relatives, and a provided a dozen other genealogical kindnesses.

One of those cousins told us about Julia McQuillan, the Black Nun of Bonamargy Friar in County Antrim. She was a legend in her day (mid-1600s), famed for the imposing figure she cut in her black vestments, and her intolerance for the improprieties of human nature. Her demands for excessive penance for transgressions were legendary even in her own time. She was also somewhat of a prophetess, prophesying about the day when carriages would travel without the use of horses, and that ships would sail the seas without the assistance of sails — clear prophecies of the automobile and steamship.

On the next page is a picture taken of my daughter Emily and me, standing next to the tombstone of Julia McQuillan. Emily refers to this as a three-generation picture!

If you're not quite ready to fly to Ireland to seek information about your ancestors, I can see a similar letter outlining your genealogical interests in

Ireland working just as well. Why not use the same tactic to see if any of the O'Shaughnessy Clan, or McCollough Clan, or Grahams, still live in or around the place you have traced your ancestor? Your ancestor, Brian McGinty lived in Donegal? Then perhaps a note like that listed above will garner a response or two from one of Brian's ancestors that still lives in the area.

So, if you are seeking Irish ancestors, give it a try. I can vouch for its success in Ireland. What's the worst thing that could happen? The main risk, as I see it, is that the letters might be tossed in the garbage by postal workers who don't want to be bothered. But what if they are delivered? What if a distant relative responds? Cousin or not, you're sure to meet some wonderful people, and you'll likely establish some long-lasting friendships. And you may find a little more out about your family than you would ever learn from sterile old records.

Surname Search

Sometimes, searching for your ancestors may seem like the proverbial search for a needle in a haystack. But there are many tools you can use to narrow your search, making the haystack much smaller. We have discussed some of those through the pages of this chapter – US records, censuses, parish and civil registration records, wills and chancery letters.

Another tool that may assist you with your search in Ireland is an under-standing of where your ancestors came from in Ireland. The Irish – perhaps more than any other people – tend to be very clannish. Generations of Irish families lived, loved, fought and died within mere miles of their birthplaces. While that may not sound particularly exotic, that Irish tendency makes genealogy research a wee bit easier.

Years ago I ran across a newspaper article that showed a map of the counties of Ireland. Within each county, Irish surnames were written. The map explained these counties were the ancient ancestral counties for each of those surnames. Through the years and through my genealogical research, I have found that map – and other books and articles I have discovered – to be right on. While it is no guarantee your ancestor didn't wander a little ways away (or a long ways away – like to America or Australia!) – it may serve as a tool to assist you in tracing your Irish ancestors.

The McQuillans, as I have noted, are a well-known County Antrim family, and branches of the family have lived in County Antrim since the 400s – that's a long time! Next door were our arch enemies, the MacDonnells and O'Cahans.

In **Appendix B**, I have provided a list of several hundred Irish surnames and the ancestral counties from which they hail. This gives you an opportunity to focus your search.

Favorite Websites for Irish Research
There are many, many genealogy websites for Ireland. Following are some of the better ones I have run across. If you run across any that aren't on this list that were particularly helpful, let me know and I'll see if I can put them in future editions.

Ancestry.com (international edition) – *www.ancestry.com*. I think we all know by now that Ancestry.com is the 800-pound gorilla for genealogy websites in the United States. Its holdings are vast, and they have a nice Irish set of records. As of this writing, they list the following Irish record sets:

• Ireland, Births and Baptisms, 1620 to 1911
• United Kingdom and Ireland obituary collection
• Ireland, Civil Registration Marriage Index, 1845 to 1958
• Ireland, Civil Registration Birth Index, 1864 to 1958
• Ireland, Catholic Baptisms 1742 to 1881
• Irish Immigrants: New York Port Arrival Records, 1846 to 1851
• Ireland, Griffith's Valuation 1848 to 1864

And a host of other records. I am quite fond of the Ancestry.com Irish collection – a great deal of research and work has gone into it. However, one of the things I have found about using Ancestry.com, is that sometimes they have records collections that are well hidden and difficult to find from within the website. Very curious. I have often searched the Ancestry.com database and card catalog for a particular type of record (say, *Irish Gravestone Inscriptions*, for example), but to no avail. So I give up and try Googling it, and lo and behold, one of the first hits that comes up is *Irish Gravestone Inscriptions* on Ancestry.com! This has happened many times to me, so I have resorted to checking at Ancestry.com a few times, but if I can't find a particular record set quickly (especially if I am seeking a records set I am almost positive they have), I just Google it, along with the word *Ancestry.com*, and will often find a link that takes me back inside Ancestry.com.

CIRCLE — *chancery.tcd.ie/*. As noted above, this is a great website launched by scholars at Trinity College in Dublin. It is an attempt to recover and make available significant information that was lost when genealogy records held in the Four Courts were destroyed. A great deal of information from many years ago is available on this site. Besides being intensely interesting for the peek it provides into life in medieval Ireland, it may also be the source of genealogical linkages you may otherwise never be able to get elsewhere.

Cyndi's List – *www.cyndislist.com*. Cyndi's List of genealogy websites has long been a useful website to visit, and provides a large number of links to Irish genealogy websites. Cyndi's List was the first genealogy mega-website I used, beginning nearly twenty years ago, so I have a soft spot in my heart for it. At the time of this writing, there were over 4,800 links to Irish-related genealogy sites.

Dennis A. Hogan's Irish Genealogy Website — *www.dennisahogan.com/ home.cfm*. I stumbled across this website while researching this book. Dennis is a professional genealogist who specializes in Irish research, and he was helpful and accommodating to me when I approached him and asked if I could use some information he had put together about Irish genealogy (see **Appendix A**). If you're coming up short in your search for your Irish ancestors, Dennis may be able to help you.

FamilySearch – *www.familysearch.org* — has a number of documents and videos courses about Irish research, and all are available to the public for free. I found the following video course especially helpful in understanding Irish research: Irish Civil Registration (*broadcast.lds.org/elearning/FHD/Community/en/FamilySearch/IrelandBeginningResearch/Ireland_Civil_Registration/ Player.html*). At the time of this writing, it was one of 145 video courses on doing Irish research (some were more focused on Irish research only, while others contained references to Irish research in videos about research in other countries). These courses can be found from the *Learn* tab on the *FamilySearch.org* home page and viewed from home.

On the *Learn* tab, you'll also see an option for *Research Wiki*. If you click that, and enter *Irish research* in the *Search* box, you'll be treated to (as of this writing) over 600 articles on Irish research. FamilySearch.org has a nice collection of Irish records, including:

• Irish births and baptisms, 1620 to 1881
• Ireland deaths, 1864 to 1870
• Irish civil registration indexes, 1845 to 1958
• Irish marriages, 1619 to 1898

Those records collections above represent about 26 million Irish names. Along with other miscellaneous records and family histories, the Family History Library in Salt Lake City has more than 3,000 books, over 11,500 microfilms and 3,000 microfiche containing information about the people of Ireland. Virtually all of these records are available to you no matter where you live by making a visit to a Family History Center at the local LDS chapel nearest to where you live.

GENUKI —*www.genuki.org.uk/contents/*. GENUKI is a genealogy site for the United Kingdom and Ireland. The acronym comes from **GEN**ealogy of the **UK** and Ireland (you probably already figured that out!). This is a great website to begin your research in England and / or Ireland. It's well organized, easy to understand and serves as a gateway to a large number of records. And – it's free, although some of the pages lead you to subscription or pay-per-view services. It sort of reminds me of Cyndi's List – it's really more of a directed portal to other genealogy websites. It has a number of categories listed for Irish research, such as:

• Archives and Libraries
• Biographies
• Cemeteries
• Censuses
• Church Records

- Civil Records
- Directories
- Emigration and immigration
- Probate records
- Etc.

Irish Genealogy — *www.irishgenealogy.ie*. This is a great, free website that provides abstracts of a large number of Irish genealogy records. Baptism, birth, death and marriage records are all available. As of this writing, they have over 3 million pre-1900 records available to search. So far it is somewhat limited in scope – its records include church records of the Roman Catholic Church and the Church of Ireland from Counties Carlow, Cork, Kerry and Dublin City. But they are adding records all the time, and those digitized records are free to view online. The project is being funded by *Department of Arts, Heritage and the Gaeltacht* and through the work of the *Dublin Heritage Group* and *Kerry Genealogical Research Centre*. Let's hope they continue funding the project!

Irish Origins — *www.irishorigins.com/signup-info.aspx*. This is one of the larger Irish genealogy subscription services websites, and I really like them. They offer access to over 80 million records, including censuses, wills, birth, marriage and death records, burial and cemetery records, etc.

Unlike several of their competitors (see *Roots Ireland* below) Irish Origins allows pay–per–view, 72-hour, monthly and annual subscriptions. You can get a combined British and Irish subscription or if you're only interested in Irish genealogy, you can get an Ireland-only subscription. Costs as of this writing are:

	72-hour	Monthly	Annual
British only	£7.00	£9.50	(not available)

| Irish only | £6.00 | £9.50 | (not available) |
| Combination | £8.00 | £10.50 | £55.00 |

(Note these prices are in British pounds (£), not euro ( ) or dollars.)

National Archives — *www.census.nationalarchives.ie.* If you wish to view the 1901 or 1911 censuses for Ireland, this is the place to be. Census pages are initially presented as transcripts (especially helpful with poor handwriting or Gaelic names), but you can also view the actual images online – a great deal.

Public Record Office of Northern Ireland (PRONI) — *www.nidirect.gov.uk/index/do-it-online/leisure-home-and-community-online/research-your-family-and-local-history.htm.* The official website for records in Northern Ireland has been a great and helpful website as I have researched my Northern Ireland ancestors. I like their organization, find it user friendly, and am pleased with the various collections they have for genealogists.

Roots Ireland — *www.rootsireland.ie/.* Roots Ireland is another large database of Irish records. They boast over 19 million Irish records online, including birth, marriage and death records, baptismal, census and cemetery records. They even had a few passenger lists thrown in for good measure. It is a pay-per-view sight – you have to purchase credits that will allow you to view records. They have several pricing schemes, allow bulk purchasing of credits, etc.

Irish World – *www.historyfromheadstones.com.* This is a great website for searching headstone transcriptions. They have transcribed over 50,000 headstones contained in Ulster cemeteries, and are a great source for reviewing headstone transcriptions. There is a fee to view each inscription – 4 credits – but there is a good index, so you'll know who you're looking at before you shell out the money for viewing. The cost as of this writing is about $6.50 per image – a little steep.

Ancestry Ireland – *www.ancestryireland.com.* Ancestry Ireland offers subscribers views of around two million genealogical records, including gravestone inscriptions, birth, marriage and death records. The cost of membership is about $55 per year, which allows you to spend two credits to view images (it also provides you with 24 credits to begin your research). Without the membership, the cost to view images is 4 credits. Credits cost about $1.50 each as of this writing.

Ancestors at Rest – *www.ancestorsatrest.com* – this is a great website for finding cemetery records and tombstone inscriptions. Among other records, they have Irish and English cemetery record collections.

Google – *www.google.com.* Google is a great – but often overlooked — place for genealogical research in Ireland. Play around with your search string to see what comes up. For example, we have already established that my McQuillan Ancestors hail from County Antrim in what is now Northern Ireland. When I entered *McQuillan County Antrim Genealogy*, I received nearly 25,000 hits. Now, you and I both know that many of those hits are barely related, but many are absolutely related. For example, here are a number of the hits I got:

> **The McQuillan Clan Association** – a genealogy society in County Antrim devoted to the McQuillan clan. Included on the website are things like a history of the family, links to lineages for the McQuillan family, a McQuillan DNA project, a link to a pedigree chart that extends back to the 1200s, etc. There are even stories of legendary McQuillans (no, I am not listed there…).

McQuillan Genealogy Forum – a Genealogy.com message board dedicated to McQuillan lines and families that married into the McQuillan line.

McQuillan Wiki article – there was a Wikipedia article about a feud between the McQuillan and O'Cahan clans in Ireland.

I also found several extensive genealogy sites that provided hundreds of years of genealogical information for lines of the family that had come from Northern Ireland. One, the *McQuillans of County Fermanagh: Descendants of Mary McQuillan, 1790-1876*, provides a nice story about the history of the McQuillans in Northern Ireland, along with long lists of Mary's descendants.

If you want to narrow your search a bit, detail what you are seeking: County Antrim McQuillan marriage records, County Antrim McQuillan birth records, County Antrim McQuillan death records, etc.

First Names

Below are first names you are likely to run into as you are researching your Irish ancestors. You may wonder why I am taking the time to provide Irish names for boys and girls for you. They speak English in Ireland, right? Yes and no. Yes – most of the Irish speak English. However, there are areas of Ireland designated as *Gaeltacht* – areas where the inhabitants usually speak Gaelic – also known as the Irish language. Through the centuries since the English occupied Ireland, many of the names adopted by the Irish have English origins. Many, however, have Gaelic origins. I have told my wife that had I been as in touch with my Irish roots as I now am, at least several of our children would have carried Irish names: Maeve, Aiofe, and Siobhan for the girls and Aidan, Ciaran and Eamon for the boys are among the possibilities. (It is apparently a good thing I was happy with good old American names…my wife wasn't too sold on the fact that I liked Irish names. I *was* able to get Teague approved as one of our son's middle names, however!)

Haillí na héireann ainmneacha chéad *(Irish boys first names)*

Aedan

Breandan

Cabhan

Carrig

Cathal

Cian

Ciaran

Coilin

Colm

Conall

Conan

Cormack

Darcy

Deaglan

Diarmuid

Donal

Eamonn

Eoghan

Faolan

Fergus

Finbar

Hugh

Jarlath

Liam

Lorcan

Malachi
Niall
Oisin
Padraig
Riordan

Cailíní na héireann ainmneacha chéad (Irish girls first names)
Aine
Aiofe
Aislin
Branna
Briana
Brigid
Caitronia
Colleen (of course!)
Deirdre
Emer
Eithne / Enya
Fianna
Fiona
Fionnoula
Gael
Granuaile
Kaitlyn
Maebh
Maire
Meara
Niamh

4. TRACING YOUR BRITISH ROOTS

I really like doing Irish genealogy – in fact, I love it. But I have to admit: doing genealogy in England is a lot easier than doing it in Ireland! There are so many more British records than there are Irish records, and many more British records are online than are Irish records. This isn't only because Britain had a larger population than Ireland. There are several reasons: first, nearly a thousand years of Irish records were destroyed in the Irish Civil War in 1922. Second, the Church of England kept tremendous records for 100s of years. And finally, many organizations in England have pushed for online access to records.

SEPARATED BY A COMMON LANGUAGE

When my wife and I visited long-lost cousins in Northern Ireland, we had a delightful time. As we were leaving, one of the cousins took my wife's hand, and shaking it vigorously, said, "We're so glad you came. You are so plain and homely." For a moment we were both stunned by this seemingly insulting comment. But the broad smile on her face and the enthusiastic nods of agreement from the other Irish cousins present made us realize that in American English she was saying: "We're so glad you came. You are so down-to-earth and comfortable to be with."

That experience reinforced for us the fact that while we share a similar language with that part of the world, there are some distinct differences. Another difference is that there are still many vestiges of Gaelic in their vocabulary. [Note – the above was borrowed from another of the books written by the author – *Ireland Guide*, Open Road Publishing (alas, now out of print!)]

Okay – so you are thinking, that may be true for social greetings, but what's that got to do with British genealogy? Well, how about *strays*? Do you know what a stray is as it relates to British genealogy? How about a *marriage bann*? (And no, it has nothing to do with an irate father's adamant refusal to allow his son or daughter to enter into marriage with an undesirable person who has stolen their heart!) And let's not get into *heaping* just yet (but we will!).

One advantage you will have – or so you would think – when doing British research, is that the records will all be in English. Unlike research you may do in other countries, you will not have to learn a new language, or at least enough words to identify genealogically significant words. Notwithstanding that bonus, old English records can be nearly as difficult to read as records in other languages, owing to archaic spelling, Gothic handwriting, etc. But – still, you should be thankful you don't have to bridge the language barrier in addition to the archaic usage and script stumbling blocks.

In the 2010 US Census of the United States, roughly twenty-six million Americans indicated they were of British descent. That number was fourth behind German, African-American and Irish ancestry. So if you are of English extraction, you appear to be in good company.

British research, like research for ancestors in other countries, should first begin here in America. There are so many records available here in the US that will make your search within the British Isles much easier. Passenger lists, immigration and naturalization records, censuses, county biographies, etc., may help you pinpoint areas where in-country research needs to begin. Ignoring these records and trying to jump directly to in-country records may unnecessarily add cost and aggravation to your research.

United States Records
Let's start first here in the United States. Briefly, I'll identify a number of

sources that may ease the process of finding your ancestors in the United Kingdom. We'll look at a few samples of those records, so you'll understand the information you can glean from them. Then we'll jump to England and see what we can find there.

Family Tradition / Legend / Knowledge

Odd as this may seem, don't look past your family when seeking for clues to your ancestors' lives and records in England. Perhaps *your* father or grandfather remembers *his* father or grandfather talking about what it was like to grow up in _____ (insert name of any English city or town). My great aunt Ruth was a wonderful source of genealogical information – it seemed that all the family stories found their way to her, and she had a remarkable memory. She could regale you with the stories of her ancestors – where they came from, when they came, when they first settled and where. Anecdotes that weave a colorful tapestry of the lives of your ancestors may contain clues that will help you identify records or places to search for records.

Who is *my* great Aunt Ruth?

Don't ignore those stories – in fact, capture them, either in writing, or if possible, even through video or voice recordings. What a special treasure to have once your great Aunt Ruth is gone, not to mention the genealogical treasure and research aid it may be for you.

Ah – but here's a caution: understand that your great Aunt Ruth (or Aunt Annie, Aunt Millie, Aunt Agnes, etc.) may have mixed up her stories. Or she may have not heard it correctly in the first place. So accept the information for what it is – a clue to help you find other clues and records.

A few years ago, I had an example of that with my wonderful great Aunt Ruth. For years I had pestered her for information about my Uncle Lynn's wife, Aunt Agnes. Ruth had told me Agnes was born in Sharon Springs, Kansas. Try as I might, I could not find her birth records there. I could find her as a toddler in the census for Sharon Springs, but couldn't confirm her birth there. Then one day Ruth and I were visiting and a distant cousin was with us. I decided to ask Ruth if she was certain Agnes was born in Sharon Springs, which she confirmed. But the cousin piped up and said, "No she wasn't! She was born in Cottonwood Falls, Kansas, and her folks moved to Sharon Springs when she was a baby." So, Ruth's memory got me close – in the correct state, but about 325 miles and five or six counties away. So again – be persistent in gleaning all the information you can from aging relatives, but be judicious with its use.

United States census records
The federal censuses for 1900, 1910, 1920, 1930 and 1940 each asks a series of questions that may provide clues that will assist you in finding these British ancestors of yours. These censuses all asked whether a person had been naturalized, along with other helpful immigration-related questions. The 1920 census went a step further by requesting the year of naturalization. That last will be especially helpful, and will assist you in locating your ancestor's naturalization papers. By census, here are the immigration and naturalization questions asked (this is in addition to the questions that asked for the birth place of the individual and of his and her parents):

1900
• If an immigrant, the year of immigration to the United States.
• How long the immigrant has been in the United States.
• Is the person naturalized?

1910
• Year of immigration to the United States
• Whether naturalized or alien

• Whether able to speak English, or, if not, give language spoken.

1920

• Year of immigration to the United States
• Naturalized or alien
• If naturalized, year of naturalization

1930

• Year of immigration into the United States
• Naturalization
• Whether able to speak English

1940

• Citizenship of the foreign born
• Mother tongue (or native language) if foreign born
• Citizenship of the foreign born?

In the *Citizenship* column of these censuses, where the above questions were asked, these abbreviations were used: AL = Alien, NA = Naturalized, NR = Not Reported, PA = First Papers filed (the immigrant's declaration of intention).

As you review this information, you will be able to determine if indeed your ancestor was born in Britain (or elsewhere). Pay particular attention to the abbreviations used in the *Citizenship* column; you are particularly hopeful that you find one of the following in that column for your ancestor:

• NA = Naturalized
• PA = First Papers

Naturalized means that your ancestor may have gone through the process of completing the naturalization process. The application (called Petition for Citizenship), often had a great deal of genealogical information contained in it about the individual and his/her family. I say *may* have gone through the process, since before 1922, women received citizenship by virtue of their husband's citizenship, whether naturalized or already an American citizen. Also, minor children received citizenship by virtue of their father's citizenship. So even though the census indicates that a female ancestor may have been naturalized, she may not have completed any paperwork. Same with her minor children.

First papers means the immigrant had filed their first immigration papers, also known as *Declarations of Intention*. These papers were often filed within days of an immigrant's arrival in America. Often, however, they were not followed up on – their naturalization wasn't completed. Even at that, Declarations of Intention also have excellent genealogical data available on them.

In all of my genealogy books, I like to use my own ancestors to help identify research strategies and tactics. As stated earlier in this book, nine of my direct-line ancestors were of Irish ancestry. However, I did have two wayward lines that came through the United Kingdom – the Hudsons and the Turpins (sometimes spelled Turpen). Let's see if we can't find something about Joseph Hudson, an erstwhile member of the United Kingdom, who, along with his wife Annie and several children, moved to America. On the next page is their entry in the 1930 United States Census for Baltimore, Maryland.

The census record showed that each of the individuals in this family had been born in England. Without going any further, that helps establish a date before which the family had been living in England – at least 1918 (since Margarete was 12 years old and born in England).

Name	Age	Year Immigrated	Naturalized or Alien?	Age at FirstMarriage
Hudson, Joseph	44	1923	PA	20
Annie	46	1925	AL	22
Doris	22	1925	AL	
Joseph R.	20	1923	AL	
Margarete	12	1923	AL	

Of course, had we read just a little further over to the right, we would have learned a little more about the immigration status of this family. In what was a fairly common occurrence, it appears that part of the family came to America first, established themselves, and then sent for the remaining members of the family. Joseph, his son Joseph R. and his daughter Margarete came to America in 1923, when young Joseph R. was about 13 and Margarete was 5. Two years later, in 1925, Joseph's wife Annie and 17-year-old daughter Doris arrived.

The Naturalized or Alien column is helpful to us – it tells us that while Annie and the children are all aliens (AL), Joseph has filed his first papers (PA) – his Declaration of Intention to immigrate. None of the children have filed papers, nor has Annie. Again, that is not uncommon. Annie may be like many other English wives, and will not file her own naturalization papers, preferring instead to gain citizenship through her husband's naturalization. Same with the minor children. Except for Doris, who has already reached majority, the other children may be waiting until their father gains his citizenship, and then they too can be citizens.

Immigration & Naturalization Records

Information about most immigrants to the United States was captured in any number of immigration and naturalization documents. The first immigration or naturalization documents you are likely to find your immigrating ancestor on will most likely be *passenger lists*, also known as *ship's manifests*.

The United States government required all vessels, from a very early time in our country's history, to keep accurate logs of the passengers and crew members that traveled on their ships. In the early years of the country, very little information was kept beyond the name of the traveler, although as the years went on more and more information was gathered. When the federal government took over the immigration practice in 1906 (it was the purview of the states until that time), they standardized the forms and the process for immigration.

Between 1820 and 1920, immigrants entered the US in the following numbers at the following points:
Baltimore, MD – 1,460,000
Boston, MA — 2,050,000
Charleston, SC – 20,000
Galveston, TX – 110,000
Key West, FL – 130,000
New Bedford, MA – 40,000
New York City, NY – 32,500,000
New Orleans, LA – 710,000
Passamaquoddy, Maine – 80,000
Philadelphia, PA – 1,240,000
Portland / Falmouth, ME – 120,000
Providence, RI – 40,000
San Francisco, CA – 500,000

As you can see, the top ports in order of arrival in the United States were:
New York
Boston
Baltimore
Philadelphia
New Orleans
San Francisco

If you are looking for British immigrants, you might focus first on New York, Boston, Philadelphia and Baltimore. There are several reasons for this:

1. between those four ports, nearly 39 million immigrants arrived;
2. those four ports represented more-or-less straight shots from the ports from which the British were most likely to have left.

Having said that, since I found the Joseph Hudson family in Baltimore, Maryland, I decide to look online to see if I can find any passenger lists for Baltimore. A number of websites offer online passenger lists, and I find the Baltimore passenger lists at Ancestry.com. I check there and…nothing. Okay, well, Philadelphia is close to Baltimore, so I check there, and…nothing. Hmmm. Okay – I decide to move further north, and try New York passenger lists, again on Ancestry.com. And…no Joseph! However, I am fortunate that I notice an Annie Hudson in the New York passenger lists, so I check her out, and here is what I find:

On the *SS Carmania*, sailing from Liverpool, England on 14 February 1925 and arriving in New York on 23 February 1925, we find:

Name	Age	Last permanent Residence	Name of nearest relative in home country
Hudson, Annie	40	Barrow, England	Father, Mr. G. Harris, Barrow
Doris May	16	Barrow, England	Grandfather, Mr. G. Harris, Barrow
Joseph Robt.	14	Barrow, England	Grandfather, Mr. G. Harris, Barrow
Marguerite	7	Barrow, England	Grandfather, Mr. G. Harris, Barrow

What a find! I am still concerned I haven't yet found Joseph, the father, but this is certainly his family. A couple of important finds here:

- Annie and all the children came in 1925, not 1923. The 1930 census indicated Joseph Robert and his little sister Marguerite accompanied their father in 1923.
- We have discovered Annie's maiden name – Harris – and the first initial of her father's name: G. So often in my research, women's maiden names are sometimes difficult to uncover.
- I also know where her father lives – 75 Anson Street in Barrow-on-Furness (his address is included on the passenger list, but not above).
- Annie and her children were living in Barrow-in-Furness just prior to their departure for America. (In case you're wondering, Barrow-in-Furness is about 50 miles north of Liverpool.)

Note – don't forget to go to the second page of the passenger list – in later years, there were so many questions, entries spanned two pages. On the second page, I found the following information:

- They were going to join Annie's husband, J. Hudson.
- J. Hudson was living in Baltimore.
- Annie gave Joseph's address as being in care of Mrs. Edmundson in Sparrow's Point, Baltimore Maryland. (I should keep Mrs. Edmundson's name handy…she may be a sister, aunt, niece, grandmother, etc.)
- This was interesting: Annie said she had been to America before in 1888 (when she was about 3) and 1893 (when she was about 8) in Homestead, Pennsylvania. I should make a note of that – perhaps she has family there.

Don't forget the second page of passenger lists!

While I am pleased with this wonderful information, I am concerned I cannot find Joseph. So I try Boston passenger lists, knowing that it was also a busy port, and many ships from England landed there. And…success:

On the *SS Andania*, sailing from Liverpool, England on 3 March 1923 and arriving in New York on 14 March 1923, we find:

Name	Age	Last permanent Residence	Name of nearest relative in home country
Hudson, Joseph	37	Barrow, England	Wife, Annie Hudson 75 Anson Lane, Barrow-in-Furness, England

I also checked the 1940 census to see if Joseph and Annie were still living in Sparrow's Point, and had success. In addition, I found 30-year-old Joseph Robert living with his parents, along with his 23-year-old wife Frances. The census also showed that Joseph, Annie and Joseph Robert had all been naturalized. I checked for naturalization papers for Annie and Joseph Robert, and finding none, am assuming they used Joseph's naturalization for themselves. Joseph Robert's wife was born in Illinois.

So there we have it – we have found the entire family. In our research thus far, we've found a discrepancy – the year several of the children immigrated. But – through deductive reasoning (with a little assistance from Ancestry.com!) we were able to find all members of the family.

The next immigration or naturalization record I am going to seek for Joseph and members of his family is their naturalization papers, either their Declaration of Intention to immigrate (also called first papers) or their Petition for Citizenship.

Declarations of Intention were often filed immediately upon an immigrant's arrival in America. Petitions of Citizenship (also known as second papers) were not filed until a minimum of five years after an immigrant's arrival in

America – a government requirement. You may recall from the 1930 census that Joseph had filed his first papers, while none of the rest of the family had filed any papers.

Once again, I fired up Ancestry.com and went in search of Joseph's first or second papers. It was only moments before I found Joseph's Petition for Citizenship. Here's the information contained on that delightful genealogical instrument:

Name: Joseph Hudson

Birth date: September 19, 1886

Birth place: Barrow-in-Furness, England

Place of residence: 519 F. Street, Sparrow's Point, MD

Occupation: Machinist

Arrived: September 2, 1915 on the St. Paul

Declared Intent to Immigrate: April 28, 1924, Baltimore, MD District Court

Wife's name: Annie Hudson

Married: April 21, 1906

Wife's birth date: August 20, 1884

Wife's birthplace: Barrow-in-Furness, England

Place and date wife entered country: February 22, 1925 in Baltimore, MD

Children's names and birth dates:

• Doris, October 27, 1907, born in Barrow-in-Furness, England

• Joseph Robert, October 16, 1909, born in Barrow-in-Furness, England

• Marguerite, April 15, 1917, Barrow-in-Furness, England

Residence of children and wife: all reside with Joseph in Sparrow's Point, MD

Last foreign residence: Barrow-in-Furness, England

Place and Date immigrant entered country: March 14, 1923, Boston, Massachusetts

Witnesses: Jacob Davies and Thomas McDonough (both machinists, living in Sparrows Point, MD)

Passport Applications

As I noted in the *Tracing Your Irish Roots* chapter, passport applications can provide a wealth of genealogical information about family members for whom you are doing research. Immigrants traveled back to their countries of origin – far more than I think a lot of us realize. Lives were left, including aging parents, siblings, and sometimes even children and grandchildren. Estate matters had to be attended to, and some even left their businesses in the hands of others to run. I suppose there are as many reasons for immigrants returning to their home country as there are immigrants.

I had hoped to find a passport application for Joseph Hudson so I could share some of the information typically found on passport applications, but alas, no such luck. Not to be deterred, I decided to see if there were any other British immigrants named Hudson who had traveled abroad and had applied for a passport. Ancestry.com yielded me a great example – perhaps a namesake for the Joseph Hudson we have been following – Joseph H. Hudson. On May 31, 1921, Joseph H. Hudson applied for a United States passport. Here is the information I was able to glean from his passport:

Name: Joseph H. Hudson
Birth place: Lancashire, England
Birth date: August 27, 1857
Date of immigration: 1879
Residence: Newburyport, MA
Court of naturalization: Police Court of Newburyport, MA
Father's name: John Hudson
Father's birth place: England
Traveler's occupation: Merchant
Object of visit: Business

I thought it was interesting that he said this was his twenty-fourth trip to England since his arrival in 1879 – an average of nearly once every two years since his arrival 42 years earlier!

I learn a lot about Mr. Hudson that I might not normally have known before through his passport application. This is especially true if I hadn't been able to find his naturalization papers, or a passenger list with his name and information on it.

As you can see, some great questions were asked travelers that are helpful to genealogical researchers. Passports were not required for United States citizens until 1941; prior to that they were available and recommended, but not required (except for brief periods during the Civil War and World War I). Even at that, the National Archives has nearly two million passport applications on file for travelers between 1795 and 1925. The applications for these passports sometimes provide genealogical information.

Until the first quarter of the 20th century, the vast majority of passports (95%) were issued to men. This doesn't mean women didn't travel abroad; until the 1920s, women and children traveling with their husbands were listed on their husband's passport.

Unlike today's passports that are good for ten years (for adults), passports in the early years of the United States were valid for two years; therefore, you may find numerous passports for your ancestors.

Military Records

If your British ancestors fought in any of America's wars, military records may provide important clues to the origins of your ancestor and/or his ancestors. Following are some of the more important US military records that might provide clues that will assist you in doing research in Britain:

- **Revolutionary War pension records** – "What!?" you ask? English men having US Revolutionary War records like pension records? Remember – until the war, a significant number of the country's population was British, or at most, removed from Britain by a generation or two. Many considered themselves Americans first, Royal Subjects second, and many of these men shouldered arms against England. I discovered the pension application for my fifth great grandfather, who was 19 years old at the beginning of the Revolutionary War (prime age for soldiering!) and it included the following information:
  - His residence at the time of application
  - Birth date and place
  - The fact he was married
- **Civil War pension records** – these records often grant researchers rich rewards for their effort. I have found vital genealogical information about service men ancestors of mine as well as their spouses and children: name, date and place of birth, wife's maiden name, names and birth dates of all children under age 16, marriage date, and even the names of children and the dates they died. Many English men, or the sons of English men, fought in the Civil War, and their records help tell their story.
- **World War I draft registration cards** – World War I draft registration cards may provide information that will help you unlock your ancestor's past. All men – US citizens or not — ages 18 to 45 who were residing in the United States during the World War I years were required to complete draft registration cards. Estimates are that 98% of men complied with this requirement. These cards provided name, age, address, birth date and place, the name of someone who would always know where they were, nearest relative, immigration status, etc. Even if your British ancestor hadn't yet been naturalized (or if he never was), there is a good chance that he completed a draft registration card.

- **World War II draft registration cards** — this registration was taken in April 1942. It was for men who were born between April 28, 1877 and February 16, 1897. The government was not seeking to draft these older men (ages 45 to 64), but instead was gleaning information on the industrial skills and capacity of the workforce. They wouldn't be used for military service, but the information provided the government with an inventory of the manpower resources available at that time.

So don't overlook military records as sources of information that might provide a clue for finding that elusive British°™ ancestor of yours. You can get a more thorough treatment of this important set of records in *Quillen's Essentials of Genealogy: Mastering Census and Military Records* and *The Troubleshooter's Guide to Do-It-Yourself Genealogy.*

Since Joseph Hudson immigrated to America in 1923 and would have been between the ages of 45 and 64 at the time the World War II draft registration would have been conducted (he would have been 56 years old in 1942) I decided to check that draft registration.

A few clicks of my mouse uncovered his World War II draft registration card at Ancestry.com. Here's the information I found for him:

Name: Joseph Hudson

Residence: 519 F. Street, Sparrow's Point, Maryland

Age: 56

Birth date: September 19, 1885

Birth place: Barrow-in-Furness, England

Name of person who will always know your address: Mrs. Annie Hudson, 519 F. Street, Sparrow's Point, Maryland

(Note that Joseph's birth date is a year earlier than reported on his Petition for Citizenship.)

Because of other records we were able to find for Joseph, none of this information was new. However, had we been unable to unearth his naturalization papers, or been unable to find him on a passenger list, some of the information on his draft registration card (especially his place of birth) would have been a great find.

> Military records can yield great information on my ancestors!

United States Records Summary

Thank you for your patience in hanging with me in searching for your British roots by beginning here in the USA. Hopefully I have convinced you that overlooking US records when searching for your British ancestors may make your job unnecessarily difficult. Let's quickly review the information I have been able to glean on this shirt-tail British cousin of mine from US records:

Name: Joseph Hudson

Birth date: September 19, 1885 (one source), September 19, 1886 (one source)

Birth place: Barrow-in-Furness, England

Immigrated to US: 1923

Wife's name: Annie Hudson

Wife's maiden name: Harris

Wife's father's name and address: Mr. G. Harris, 75 Anson Street, Barrow-in-Furness, England

Wife's birth date: August 20, 1884

Wife's birthplace: Barrow-in-Furness, England

Place and date wife entered country: February 22, 1925 in Baltimore, MD

Married: April 21, 1906

Children's names and birth dates:

• Doris May, October 27, 1907, born Barrow-in-Furness, England

• Joseph Robert, October 16, 1909, born Barrow-in-Furness, England
• Marguerite, April 15, 1917, born Barrow-in-Furness, England

As you can see, the information for Joseph Hudson and his family is pretty extensive. Not only do I have a place to begin searching in England for more information about them (Barrow-in-Furness), I have also learned Annie's maiden name, the name of her father, and the place where her father is living. All great information to have in my back pocket as I head into English records, looking for more details about these Hudson ancestors of mine. Using the above information, I can focus my search around several key genealogical elements.

Key British Records
There are a number of key records available as you begin your search for your British roots. Following are some of those sources:

British censuses
Like their American cousins, the British have conducted censuses every ten years since the beginning of the 19th century (the Americans began at the end of the 18th century, with the 1790 census). Censuses were enumerated every ten years beginning in 1801. For some reason, they didn't complete a 1941 survey (they were a little busy / preoccupied at the time!). That's a shame, since genealogists in America have been thrilled with the release of the 1940 census here.

For those of you who have become familiar with doing research with US censuses, you know they can be a great assist to genealogical research. The same holds true for research in Britain, however, there are some important differences between US and British censuses. Following are some of the primary differences:
• **Questions** — the questions are similar, but different. The main questions

are the same: name, relationship to the head of household, age (there's a caveat here — see below), place of birth, etc.

- **1801 to 1831 censuses** – Many of the census records for these years were lost or destroyed. When there is information, it is like the US censuses between 1790 and 1840 – tallies of family members under the name of the head of household. Sometimes, the only information that survived for some areas are tallies – no names.

- **Dates of enumeration** – British censuses were taken in the second year of each decade: 1841, 1851, etc. Enumerations were generally in the April / May timeframe of those years.

- **Release date** — in the US, censuses are released to the public 72 years after they were enumerated; in Britain, censuses are only released after 100 years. That means the latest census available for awhile is the 1911 census.

- **Age** – in the US, the age of each individual is included. In Britain, the ages of those over 15 years of age are rounded to the nearest five years. So a family with children ages 15, 17 and 19 could show them as aged 15, 15 and 20. (Note – this was the instruction for enumerators, but I have reviewed many British census records, and many of them appear to have the exact (unrounded) age. But I am always suspicious of dates that are in fact multiples of 5 – not knowing for certain whether that was a person's real age or rounded age.

- **Indexes** – Indexes are not always readily available for the British censuses. Some subscription services have indexes, some do not. Ancestry.com's international edition, for example, has indexes available for the 1841 through 1901 censuses. British Origins, another subscription site, only had 1841, 1861, and 1871 indexes available at the time of this writing.

- **All persons** – The first British census to list all individuals in a household by name was the 1841 census. (In the US, the first census to list all individuals was 1850, so the Brits are ahead of us on that one!) British censuses prior to that simply provide tallies of the household under the head of household name, similar to the US censuses prior to 1850.

British census terms you may not be aware of:
- *Stray* – a person appearing in a record who is not from the place of enumeration.
- *Summary Books* – sometimes you'll run into Summary Books. These books just provide the name of the head of house with how many males and females are living in the house, similar to US censuses from 1790 to 1840, except age ranges are not listed.
- *Workhouse* – a house built specifically to house poor or destitute people.
- *Heaping* – the tendency of some enumerators to round ages, especially those of children, to a number divisible by two (14, 16, 18, 20, etc.).
- *Spinster* – a single, unmarried woman.

Watch out for heaping and strays!

So let's take some of the information we gleaned from US records and see if we can't find more information on my British cousins. If you'll recall, here is information we learned about the Joseph Hudson family:
- The family came to America in the 1920s;
- All family members were born in Barrow-in-Furness, England;
- The family lived in Barrow-in-Furness, England prior to immigrating;
- Annie's maiden name is Harris, and her father's name is Mr. G. Harris;
- Doris was born in 1907, Joseph Robert in 1909 and Marguerite in 1917;
- Joseph was born in 1885 or 1886, and Annie was born in 1884;
- Joseph and Annie were married in 1906.

All these bits of data will help us take the next steps in our genealogical journey – but this time in a land far away and in non-US records. Here are things to consider about that information we gleaned from US records:

- Since the family came to the US in the 1920s, that means we may be able to find them in the 1911 and 1901 British censuses (remember – British census records aren't released for 100 years, so the 1921 census won't be available for awhile).
- The fact that all family members were born in Barrow-in-Furness and that is the town from which they all immigrated allows us to search there.
- Knowing Annie's maiden name and her father's first initial may allow us to locate her and the family she grew up in.
- With birth dates of 1885-ish and 1884, we may be able to find Joseph and Annie as children in the 1891 and 1901 British censuses with their respective families.
- Since Joseph and Annie were married in 1906, we may be able to find them as a couple, beginning their young family (Doris was born in 1907 and Joseph Robert in 1909) in the 1911 census.

I was able to locate the 1911 British census through Ancestry.com and British Origins. Searching in Barrow-in-Furness for the Joseph and Annie Hudson family I find a happy little family:

Names	Age	Years Married	Birthplace
Joseph Hudson	25	5	Barrow-in-Furness
Annie Hudson	27	5	Barrow-in-Furness
Doris May Hudson	3		Barrow-in-Furness
Joseph Robert Hudson	1		Barrow-in-Furness

The record also indicates – sad day – that Annie had borne three children, only two of whom were living.

Filled with optimism, I decide to see if I can find Joseph and Annie as children in their parents' homes in the 1901 census. Since Joseph was born in August and Annie in September, and censuses were enumerated in April,

I will look for Joseph as a 14 or 15 year old (his birth date was listed in US records as 1885 and 1886), and Annie as a 16 year old in the 1901 census. Annie should be in a Harris family group. Again, since all the records I have (US as well as British) indicate Joseph and Annie were both born in and lived in Barrow-in-Furness, I'll check there again. Here's what I found:

Names	Age	Birthplace
Robert Hudson	48	Oxfordshire, Oxford
Emma Hudson	52	Oxfordshire, Oxford
Albert Hudson	17	Lancashire, Barrow-in-Furness
Joseph Hudson	15	Lancashire, Barrow-in-Furness
Lizzie Hudson	13	Lancashire, Barrow-in-Furness

This looks like the family we are seeking. There could be other Joseph Hudsons, but a search of the area turns up no others, so I feel pretty good that I have located the correct family.

Here's what I found when I searched for Annie and her family:

Names	Age	Birthplace
George Harris	50	Coventry
Eugene Harris	49	Leicester
George Harris	21	Lancashire, Barrow-in-Furness
Annie Harris	17	Lancashire, Barrow-in-Furness
Daniel Harris	16	Lancashire, Barrow-in-Furness
Hetta Quinney	24	Staffordshire Walsall
Arthur Quinney	30	Lancashire, Barrow-in-Furness
John Quinney	4	Lancashire, Barrow-in-Furness

Again, there could be more than one Harris family in Barrow-in-Furness with a 17-year-old daughter named Annie, but a search didn't turn another one up. Also listed with this family is the Quinney family. They are living with the George Harris family, and Hetta is listed as his daughter, Arthur his son-in-law and John as his grandson. The 1911 census shows Annie's mother's name as *Eugenia*, more probable than *Eugene*. (One minor pause – if Annie was born in September 1884, as we suspect, she would not yet have turned 17 during as of April 1901, when the census was enumerated.)

A couple of things about Annie's family. You see that Hetta is an elder daughter, and she was born in Staffordshire. Annie and all her siblings were born in Barrow-in-Furness, so that indicates that sometime between Hetta's birth in about 1877 and her brother George's birth in 1880, the family moved to Barrow-in-Furness. I followed

> **Be prepared to use my best detective instincts when researching older records.**

the thread of the Robert Hudson family quite a ways back along the family tree – but I won't take space here to display it. But among other things, I found the following:

• There is another daughter, two years older than Albert, named Elizabeth;
• Lizzie (as shown in the 1911 census), was named Eliza A.;
• Robert Hudson (Joseph's father) was the son of William and Elizabeth Hudson (and he died in 1800).
• Joseph's great grandfather (Robert's grandfather) was Benjamin Hudson, born in 1800 or 1801.

I was able to ferret out all this information because I was able to begin with some pretty solid data from US records, and my journey took me to just shy of the end of the 18th century and five generations from me.

I was curious whether any of the Hudson families I was researching followed the patronymics / naming patterns I listed in *The Basics* chapter, and the answer is…nope. So, as I say, families didn't always follow those patterns, but sometimes did. I did notice that the use of brother's, father's and grandfather's names were used liberally from generation to generation in this family, but no discernible pattern was evident to me.

Where to find British Census Records

Like US records, British census records continue to come online. Some of the best places I have identified to find British census records are at Ancestry.com, British Origins.com, The Genealogist, and FamilySearch.org. There are a number of other places available also – just Google *England Census online.*

Civil Registration

Civil registration of birth, marriage and deaths began in England in July 1, 1837, and in 1855 in Scotland. Indexes for these superb records are kept in book form in the Family Records Centre in London. You can see an index of the records they have at *www.FindMyPast.co.uk/home.jsp.* Records are also available at *freebmd.rootsweb.com.* The former website is a subscription service, but the latter is free. I'd suggest you start with the last one! FamilySearch.org also has many of these records online. Many are transcribed, some have images available, and still others have links to pay-per-view or subscription partners.

After my search through the censuses of England and identifying various and sundry relatives of Joseph Hudson, who we have been following in this chapter, I turned to online birth, death and marriage records. Using several online sources (*Ancestry.com, FamilySearch.org, BritishOrigins.com, freebmd.rootsweb.com, TheGenealogist.co.uk*) and message boards, I was able to find a number of birth and burial dates of individuals listed earlier in this chapter. Some of the records were exquisite in their penmanship and elegance. The burial record for Benjamin Hudson, which I found online in the Warwickshire County Record Office, Warwick, England (Warwickshire

Anglican Registers) shows that Benjamin Hudson, the fifth great grandfather of Joseph Hudson, was buried on April 6, 1800. I also found the death record for Benjamin's brother Miles, who was buried just the year before Benjamin, on April 1, 1799.

English Marriage Records

I think this is a good time to discuss marriage records in England. As you poke and prod around English records, you are certain to run across a few different terms that are associated with marriage in England:
• Allegations
• Bonds
• Banns
• Licenses

Allegations are statements or affidavits declaring the marriage being entered into was legal in the eyes of God and the law. It was sometimes signed by both the bride and the groom, but often the groom made the allegation for both parties. Allegations were only used by those who applied for marriage licenses; they were not used by couples who were married by banns.

Bonds provided for a financial penalty if the allegation as to the legitimacy of a marriage proved to be false. It was generally signed by the groom and his bondsman. The bondsman was usually a close friend or relative. Bonds were only used by those who applied for marriage licenses; they were not used by couples who were married by banns. Marriage bonds were common between the 1600s and 1823, when they ceased being used with allegations. Only allegations continued. If you run across a bond record and a sum is entered on the record, that is the penalty for falsehood, not the cost of the bond.

Banns were nothing more than the public announcement in church that a man and woman intended to marry. It was to be read over the pulpit

> Marriage bann = public announcement of an intent to marry.

("called") three consecutive Sundays prior to the wedding. Parishioners were invited to inform the clergyman if they knew of any reason the marriage would be objectionable: under-age participants, marrying a relation that was considered too close, or one of the parties was already married.

Licenses were, well, licenses to marry. They were also issued by the Church, but could be used when banns couldn't. Banns, for example, couldn't be "called" (announced) during Lent, but a marriage license could be procured during that time. While bonds and allegations became the property of the Church, licenses were given to the bride and groom, and few have survived. But you will often find them recorded in Marriage Registers.

A caution: A number of these records will list the ages of the bride and groom as 21 or over. That could mean 21 or 91, so don't get thrown a curve if you are looking for a 28-year old groom and see that *21 or older* entry.

Just because a bann was called, or a license, bond and allegation were made, is no guarantee that the marriage took place. In olden days, as now, brides and grooms got cold feet, parents, siblings or friends dissuaded their loved one from the marriage, or a potential partner died.

As you might assume, participants in marriage who were younger than 21 needed parental permission to marry, and their names will be on any marriage document or record. The legal age for marriage in England was 16, although young people under age 21 needed their parents' approval.

So, you ask, where might such marriage documents be found? They may be online if you are lucky, but more likely, they will most often be kept in the local county archives. As an example, Lancashire County, the county where Barrow-in-Furness is located (where the Joseph Hudson family was from), holds marriage bonds and allegations and marriage bann books for the following years: 1615, 1633-1634, 1636, 1642, 1648-1854 and 1861. Other counties have more records, some have fewer, some have none.

If you are seeking marriage information for a couple, you can contact the local county archives and see if they have information about them. When requesting copies of marriage banns, bonds, allegations, etc., provide all the information you have. For example, if you were seeking marriage information on Joseph and Annie Hudson, you would provide the following information:

Husband's name: Joseph Hudson

Wife's name (maiden name if you know it): Annie Harris

Marriage date: April 21, 1906 (if you don't know the exact date, you can provide a range: approx. 1902 to 1907)

Parish: Barrow-in-Furness

Husband's father's name: Robert Hudson

Wife's father's name: George Harris

Parish Registers

Prior to the beginning of civil registration (which officially began on July 1, 1837), the primary vital records were kept by the Church of England (which you'll recall, was – and still is — the official established church in England). Between 1754 and 1837, the only marriages recognized by the Crown government were those marriages performed in the Church of England. Even though your ancestors may not have been Church of England members, if they wanted to be legally married, they had to do so in the Church of England. The only exceptions granted were for Jews and Quakers. Burials of non-Church of England members were also often recorded in Church of England records if the individual's non-Church of

England church (called non-conformist or dissenter churches, or the Catholic Church) didn't have burial grounds.

Records for individuals who were not members of the Church of England may be in Church of England parish records.

If you recall your history, King Henry VIII separated from the Catholic Church in 1534 and established the Church of England. The earliest Church of England parish records date to 1535. Even though civil registration began in 1837, many vital records are still kept by the Church of England. Prior to 1754, baptisms, burials and marriages were all kept in the same record.

Prior to the beginning of civil registration, several governmental attempts were made to get record keeping started in the United Kingdom. A law was passed in 1538 requiring the recording of baptisms, marriages and burials. After Sunday meetings, clerics were required by the law to record all events in a parchment book. Clergymen disdained the law, and resented the extra cost (apparently parchment was not cheap!) and effort required. While some parishes began keeping records, others simply ignored the statute. Still others started and then stopped. Hopefully, your ancestors lived in a parish that participated continuously from the earliest years.

By the time Queen Elizabeth I ascended to the throne in 1597, many parishes weren't keeping records, so she re-instituted the statute, again with mixed success.

As part of the modernization effort and doubtless to make it easier for churchmen to keep the law, special pre-printed parish register books were produced, with standardized forms included for births, marriages and deaths. That helped somewhat, and standardized the information collected.

In 1754, the *Marriage Act of 1753* went into effect. Also known as *Lord Hardwicke's Marriage Act*, it did several things. First of all, it was:

An Act for the better preventing of clandestine marriage.

That was actually part of the title! Clandestine marriages must have been a real problem in the mid-18th century.

In addition to the prevention of clandestine marriages, the Act altered the way parish records were kept. Prior to that time, baptism, marriage and death / burial records were all kept in the same books. With Lord Hardwicke's statute, marriage records were required to be kept in separate marriage books.

In 1812, Roses' Act was instituted. It's main effort was to standardize the information required for baptisms and burials. Beginning in 1812, the following information had to be recorded for each of the following events:

Baptisms
• Name of child;
• Name of both parents (although not necessarily the mother's maiden name – darn!);
• Date of the baptism;
• Place of birth;
• Father's occupation;
• Family's residence.

Burials
• Names of deceased;
• Age of deceased;
• Date of burial;

• Occupation or rank of the deceased.

The proffered reason for Rose's Act was:

> ...amending the manner and form of keeping and of preserving Registers of Baptisms, Marriages, and Burials of His Majesty's subjects in the several parishes and places in England, will greatly facilitate the proof of pedigrees of persons claiming to be entitled to real or personal estates, and otherwise of great public benefit and advantage.

Strangely, assisting genealogists was not listed as one of the main reasons for the Act – but we all benefit nevertheless!

In addition, Rose's Act standardized the information required for marriages:
• Date of marriage
• First and surnames for bride and groom
• Whether bachelor or spinster, widower or widow
• Age of bride and groom
• Parish of residence of bride and groom
• Occupation of husband
• Father's first and surname
• Father's occupation or rank
• Signatures of bride and groom
• Whether the marriage was by banns or license
• Signature of witness(es)

Isn't all this just fascinating?!

Just to see if I could find a marriage bann from the 1700s, I set out to search. I didn't have to search long. Within probably less than a minute on Ancestry.com, I found the following entries:

March 23, 1724

Edward Simmons of the parish of St. Savior, Southwork in the County of Surry, widower, and Mary Marshall of the same parish, spinster.

March 24, 1724

Thomas Edwin of this parish (St. James), bachelor, and Esther Hudson of the parish of St. Benedict near Paul's Wharf, London, Spinster

So – both of those entries were made on March 23 and March 24, 1754 in the Islington, Clerkwell St. James Parish Book of Banns. They appeared as handwritten entries on a page of the Parish Book of Marriage Banns and Licenses. Interestingly, they were the *last* completely handwritten entries in the book – I suspect because the following day the Marriage Act of 1753 went into effect – on March 25, 1754. And in fact, the Parish Book of Marriage Banns and Licenses for Islington, Clerkwell, St. James then promptly changed – its pages were pre-typed so that the clergyman just had to fill in a few blanks. Following are a couple of the entries. Those items *in italics* were the portions that were handwritten by the clergyman:

> *Thomas Watts* of [*this*] *Parish, bachelor,* and *Jane Fawcett* of [*the*] *same parish, spinster,* married in [*this*] Church by [*License*] this [*twenty-first*] day of *November* in the year one thousand *seven* hundred and *fifty four* by me *John Doughty [Minister].*

> This marriage was solemnized between us (*signatures of Thomas and Jane*)

In the presence of (*signatures of two witnesses: N. G. Watts and Sheffield Young*)

The pre-printed text above allowed for the minister to record marriages by both bann and license. When the marriage was by bann, the same form could be used. However, in the same book were pre-printed pages specifically for marriage banns. (It isn't clear to me why the clergyman would use the non-bann form for marriage banns. I don't know if it was done in error, or if he had the choice.) Here's a transcription of one:

Banns of marriage between *Lancelot Taylor of this Parish, bachelor,* and *Martha Green of St. Katharine's of London, spinster*

Were published on the three Sundays underwritten: *by Art Campbell PW*

That is to say, on Sunday the *28th of April, 1754 by Art Campbell, Curate*

On Sunday, the *5th of May, 1754 by Art Campbell, Curate*

On Sunday, *the 12th day of May, 1754 by Art Campbell, Curate*

It was fascinating to study these handwritten records that were over 250 years old! As mentioned above, I was able to access these records from Ancestry.com, as well as FindMyPast.com.

By the way, can you imagine how excited Lancelot and his fiancé Martha must have been as they sat in the congregation on April 28, May 5 and May 12, and heard their marriage banns called over the pulpit!? Pretty exciting days for them, I imagine!

Returning to the Joseph and Annie Hudson family we've been tracking since early in this chapter, I thought I would try to find more information from parish records:

> Recorded banns provide important information about married couples.

1.Birth information about at least one of their children, and

2. Information about their child who died young.

As excited as I was about being able to trace that family from US census records to British census records – please remember these are records that contain genealogical information recorded many years after the actual event – they are considered secondary sources of genealogical information. A birth record, however, recorded at the time of the child's birth would be considered a primary source, as would the entry of a marriage in a recorder's book.

To search for these items, I decided to begin with #1, first, because, well, #1 comes before #2, but also because I suspected it might be an easier search. With the censuses, I had some idea about when the Hudson children were born. I decided to try and find the birth information about Marguerite Hudson, born April 15, 1917, according to Joseph's Petition for Citizenship. But I suspect fathers were as good 100+ years ago about remembering details like birth dates as they are today...and their memories are often fraught with error!

I decided to use Ancestry.com, so went to their English births, marriages and death records. In the *Search* section, I enter Marguerite Hudson's name, the year 1917 for her birth, and that she was born in Barrow-in-Furness, England. I immediately located her in a birth index for Barrow-in-Furness. Had I not known before, I would have learned quickly that between 1837 and 1984, the British recorded their births in the quarters of each year:

- January, February, March 1917
- April, May, June 1917
- July, August September 1917
- October, November, December 1917

Within moments, I was able to locate Ms. Marguerite Hudson, whose mother's maiden name was Harris, in the April-May-June index for 1917. Score! Looks like Dad may have been right after all. (Sorry for doubting you, Joseph.) Now, if I can't find the parish records for Barrow-in-Furness online, I can order a copy of her actual birth record for £9.25 from the British National Archives (*www.nationalarchives.gov.uk/documentsonline*). (For the record, I looked, but could not find any parish records from Barrow-in-Furness online.)

So now I decide to search for the lost Hudson child. Here's the information that will assist me to narrow my search:

Father: Joseph Hudson

Mother: Annie Harris Hudson

Marriage date: April 21, 1906

Other children's names and birth dates:

- Doris May, October 27, 1907, born Barrow-in-Furness, England
- Joseph Robert, October 16, 1909, born Barrow-in-Furness, England
- Marguerite, April 15, 1917, born Barrow-in-Furness, England
- **1911 Census** – stated that Annie had been the mother of three children, two of whom were living.

So, considering all this information, here's what I think:

I am going to give Joseph and Annie the benefit of the doubt, and decide they were very good and didn't have a child sooner than nine-ish months after their wedding date: April 1906. That would be January 1907. But Doris was born in October 1907, so while it's physically possible (I guess!), it's not probable Annie had a baby in April and then had one nine months later.

As stated above, the 1911 census says Annie had borne three children, but one had died. At the time of the census, which was enumerated on April 2, 1911, Annie was 27 years old, Doris was 3 and little Joseph Robert was 1. Hmmm, so that means either Annie had a baby between Doris and Joseph Robert – in 1908 – or she had a child between Joseph Robert's birth in October 1909 and the enumeration date – April 2, 1911.

Even though Annie could have squeezed in another baby in between Doris and Joseph Robert, I am going to scour records first between July 1910 (nine months after Joseph Robert's birth) and April 1911.

After searching, I was unable to find the deceased child in the birth records, for a couple reasons. Turns out, the surname Hudson is nearly as common in turn-of-the-twentieth-century Lancashire County, England as Smith is in America (or at least it seemed that way anyway!). And – the birth register indexes until 1910 only included the surname, forename (first name), District, volume and page number – but *not* the mother's maiden name. That element appeared in 1911! I found a couple of Hudson children born between July 1910 and April 2, 1911 who might qualify as the child we are seeking, but there was no certainty. (But you'll be pleased to know that during my search for the deceased child, I did find the birth records of both Doris and Joseph Robert!) I also checked death indexes for the area, with no luck. It made me sad not to be able to find and reunite this little one with his / her family. I'll have to keep searching.

One thing to consider – it is possible that Annie, age 27 in 1911, and, according to the 1930 US census, married at age 22 to Joseph, may have been married before, and had a child from that marriage that passed away. Or – the child could have been illegitimate. Many options to consider. But I'll keep looking! I should also consider that the deceased child may have been a twin to Doris or Joseph Robert.

Most parish records are no longer kept in the parishes – many (most) have been forwarded to the local County Record Office and the National Archives in London. The Society of Genealogists, FamilySearch.org and BritishOrigins.com also have collections available for your perusal.

Parish records are frequently centralized in a County Records Office.

I have provided a list of the County Record Offices of England in **Appendix C**. Along with the names of each county, I have included the website for easy access.

Search Ancestry.com, BritishOrigins.com and FamilySearch.org as well, as they often have collections that will provide information.

Wills & Probate Records

England offers a rich supply of wills and probate records. Some wills are 1,000 years old! Wills in England, like wills in any society, provide interesting and informative input for genealogical researchers. Generally speaking, the wills you will find in England will be for the landed gentry. They will have at least the following information:

• Name of the testator

• Beneficiaries, which may include any members of his family

• Witnesses (pay attention to these – they may be family members)

• Name(s) of the executor(s) (could be a member of the family – often an eldest son, brother or father)

- Address of the testator
- Date the will was made
- Date the will was probated

As you can see, this information may shed a great deal of light on a family at a certain point in time. It can identify spouse and children, perhaps even grandchildren, nieces and nephews and others.

Personally, I like to research wills because they regularly paint a picture of the family, their lives and the things they placed value on at the time. They help enrich my understanding of these ancestors of mine. Consider the following will I found on *British Origins* from about the time of the Revolutionary War (I have retained the original spelling):

> John Jewer of Tongham, Seale, yeoman 30 Nov 1772

> All my copyhold messuages and land in manor of Farnham and all rest of estate to my friends John Steer of Farnham, bricklayer and Richard Attfield of Worplesdon, farmer, execs. in trust to permit my wife Sarah Jewer to have rents etc. and use of household goods in her widowhood and then to sell land, etc. and from money raised invest £100 and pay interest to my daughters Sarah and Ann and to bring up my grandchildren son and daughter of my daughter Mary, deceased; also £100 between my daughters Sarah, Elizabeth and Ann and also residue; if my wife remarries to her £10.

> Witnesses: John Tanner; Richard Tanner; George Russell
> Proved: 25 May 1775 to execs.

So – here's what I glean from this will of John Jewer:
- The will was written in 1772;

- It was proved May 25, 1775 – so John died between 11/30/1772 and 5/24/1775;
- John lived in Farnham;
- His wife's name was Sarah, and she was alive on May 25, 1775;
- He had four daughters: Mary, who had died, Sarah, Elizabeth and Ann;
- His deceased daughter Mary had a son and daughter;
- It was witnessed by John and Richard Tanner, and George Russell.

A great find for this family! If this was a family I was researching, I would see if I could find out more about the three witnesses. Were they sons-in-law? Perhaps brothers-in-law? Nephews? Certainly worth taking a little time to look into.

And where do I find such intriguing documents? Try the British National Archives (*www.nationalarchives.gov.uk/documentsonline/wills.asp*), British Origins (*www.britishorigins.com*), Ancestry.com, FamilySearch.org and The Genealogist (*www.thegenealogist.co.uk*) . The cost for wills and other probate records from the British National Archives is £9.25 (about $15 as of this writing).

Registration Districts

For genealogical research between 1837 and 1874, registration districts are one of the first bits of geographical information you'll need to locate your British ancestor's information. You can determine the registration district a particular county or parish was in by going to *www.ukbmd.org.uk/genuki/places/index.html*. That website allows you to search alphabetically by registration district or parish.

Favorite Websites for British Research

Following are websites that will be helpful as you venture into the British Isles in search of your ancestors:

Ancestry.com

Ancestry.com's international subscription edition includes an extensive British collection, including nearly 200 collections, such as:

• United Kingdom and Ireland obituary collection
• England and Wales birth index 1837 to 1915
• England and Wales marriage index 1916 to 2005
• England and Wales Censuses (1841 to 1901)
• London marriage banns, 1754 to 1921
• Bedfordshire, England: Parish and Probate Records
• Berkshire, England: Parish and Probate Records
• Buckinghamshire, England: Parish and Probate Records
• Caithness, Scotland: Parish and Probate Records

And so on and so forth. I am quite fond of the Ancestry.com British collection – a great deal of research and work has gone into it. However, one of the things I have found about using Ancestry.com, is that sometimes they have records collections that are well hidden and difficult to find from within the website. Very curious. I have often searched the Ancestry.com database and card catalog for a particular type of record (say, *Irish Gravestone Inscriptions*, for example), but to no avail. So I give up and try Googling it, and lo and behold, one of the first hits that comes up is *Irish Gravestone Inscriptions* on Ancestry.com! This has happened many times to me, so I have resorted to checking at Ancestry.com a few times, but if I can't find a particular record set quickly (especially if I am seeking a records set I am almost positive they have), I just Google it, along with the word *Ancestry.com*, and will often find a link that takes me back inside Ancestry.com.

Ancestors at Rest – *www.ancestorsatrest.com* – this is a great website for finding cemetery records and tombstone inscriptions. Among other records, they have Irish and English cemetery record collections.

British National Archives — *www.nationalarchives.gov.uk/documentsonline/ wills.asp*. This website is the United Kingdom's equivalent of the National Archives and Records Administration (NARA) in the United States. This is the place you'll find many genealogical records for the United Kingdom. Birth, marriage and death records are found here. They offer many indexes online, but few of the actual records can be viewed online. Unfortunately, it's not cheap to get records; for US residents, the cost is £9.25 (~ $15 as of this writing) per certificate requested (that covers standard mail service). You could pay for an Ancestry.com subscription pretty rapidly if you can find copies of birth, marriage or death records in their collections!

You can order records online, or if you have a penchant for waiting long periods of time, you can request them via the postal service by writing to:

General Register Office
PO Box 2
Southport, Merseyside PR8 2JD

Whether your request is online or via letter, provide as much information as you know, but at a minimum, you must provide:
• Surname
• Forename (first name)
• Event year (birth, marriage, death or burial)

Indexes are kept by year and quarter and alphabetically by surname.

British Origins — *www.britishorigins.com*. This is one of the better websites for British records, and I really like them. They offer access to over 70 million records that range from 1209 to 1948 – that's a wide range of years! Their records include censuses, wills, birth, marriage and death certificates, burial and cemetery records, etc.

British Origins allows 72-hour, monthly and annual subscriptions. You can get a combined British and Irish subscription or if you're only interested in Irish genealogy, you can get an Ireland-only subscription. Costs as of this writing are:

	72-hour	Monthly	Annual
British only	£7.00	£9.50	(not available)
Irish only	£6.00	£9.50	(not available)
Combination	£8.00	£10.50	£55.00

Note these prices are in British pounds (£), not euro (€) or dollars.

Following is a sampling of the collections available through British Origins:
• England and Wales 1841 census
• England and Wales 1861 census
• England and Wales 1871 census
• Dorsey, Surrey and London marriage records, 1500 through 1856
• York marriage bonds, 1613 to 1839
• National Wills index

And that's all just a sampling. Doesn't it just make you want to dive right in?

Cyndi's List – *www.cyndislist.com.* Cyndi's List of genealogy websites has long been a useful website to visit, and provides a large number of links to British genealogy websites. Cyndi's List was the first genealogy mega-website I used, beginning nearly twenty years ago, so I have a soft spot in my heart for it. At the time of this writing, there were over 2,300 links to British-related genealogy sites.

Find My Past – *www.FindMyPast.co.uk* is another of the British services available to research your British ancestors. They offer subscription services

There are many great genealogy websites for British research.

(£69.95 for six months, £109.95 for one year) or you can purchase credits that you can then use on a pay-per-view system. Credits cost £24.95 for 280 credits, and must be used within one year. Or you can get 60 credits for £6.95, and those must be used within 90 days. Records cost 5 to 30 credits (most in the 5- to 10-credit range) to view. They boast over 750 million records.

English Parish Registers — *www.british-genealogy.com/parish-registers/english-registers.html.* I stumbled across this website while searching for some ancestors' birth records and found it to be easy to use and with a pretty good collection.

FamilySearch.org – *www.familysearch.org* has a number of documents and videos courses about British research, and all are available to the public for free. I found two great video courses that were helpful in learning and understanding British research. They are located at *www.familysearch.org/learningcenter/results.html?q=british%20research.* They represented a short beginner's series; the first is called *Principle Sources for British Research, pre-1837,* and the second is *Principle Sources for British Research, post-1837.* (Note – if you search for these videos by title, be sure to misspell the first word in the title – *Principle,* instead of using the word they should have used: *Principal.*) Each video is around thirty minutes long. At the time of this writing, they were two of 154 video courses on doing British research (some were focused solely on British research, while others contained references to British research in videos about research in other countries).

These courses can be found from the *Learn* tab on the *FamilySearch.org* home page. At the time of this writing, there are about 300 million names in FamilySearch's various British collections. So this would be a pretty good place to go when searching for your British ancestors.

FamilySearch.org has a very large collection of British records, including:
• English births and christenings, 1538 to 1975
• British deaths and burials, 1538 to 1991
• British marriages, 1538 to 1973

As a bonus, from the Home page at FamilySearch.org, on the *Learn* tab, you'll also see an option for *Research Wiki*. If you click that, and enter *British research* in the *Search* box, you'll be treated to (as of this writing) over 3,600 articles on British research.

Society of Genealogists Library — *www.sog.org.uk.* I ran across this site when researching British records at FamilySearch.org. FamilySearch has partnered with SOG to show the images of a number of British records collections currently held by the LDS Church. It is a subscription website, but the subscription isn't too bad — £10.00 one-time charge plus £29.95 for one year's membership. That allows you online access to their records, plus free access to the library in London should you venture to London to do research there.

The Genealogist — *www.thegenealogist.co.uk/.* This is a great England-based genealogy website. It provides online access to many of the records we've focused on in this book: census records, parish records (birth, baptism, marriage, death, burial), and many other records. Like several of the websites mentioned in this section, it is a subscription site. They have a number of pricing packages, ranging from entry-level access to pretty full access. There is a good comparative tool on the London County Record Office website: *www.ancestor-search.info/RSH-Pay%20Sites.htm* that compares The Genealogist's costs and offerings to Ancestry.com and

FindMyPast.com. Their packages range from £14.95 to £24.95 for a quarterly subscription to annual subscriptions that run from £54.95 to £134.50. (Note – these are in British Sterling, not US dollars.)

GENUKI — *www.genuki.org.uk/contents/*. GENUKI is a genealogy site for United Kingdom and Ireland. The acronym comes from **GEN**ealogy of the **UK** and Ireland (you probably already figured that out!). This is a great website to begin your research in England and / or Ireland. It's well organized, easy to understand and serves as a gateway to a large number of records. And – it's free, although some of the pages lead you to subscription or pay-per-view services. It sort of reminds me of Cyndi's List – it's really more of a directed portal to other genealogy websites. It has a number of categories listed for British research, such as:

• Archives and Libraries
• Biographies
• Cemeteries
• Censuses
• Church Records
• Civil Records
• Court Records
• Directories
• Emigration and immigration
• Land and Property
• Probate records
• Public Records
• Etc.

Online Parish Clerks (Genealogy) — *www.onlineparishclerks.org.uk/*. This is a great website I ran across that could be of great help to you if you have ancestors in the following English counties: Cornwall, Devon, Dorset, Essex, Hampshire, Lancashire, Somerset, Sussex, Warwickshire, or Wiltshire.

Each of these counties has parish clerks who will do research for you in their county without a fee. A blurb at the end of the website tells you how they got their start:

> The idea originated in 2000 at a Cornish pub when three friends were discussing their genealogy interests. It spread via the Cornish Mailing Lists and family researchers volunteered to take on a parish. Currently several other Counties are covered by similar schemes.

The site provides the names and contact information for these parish clerks, friends of genealogy!

Google – *www.google.com*. Google is a powerful search engine, and can often provide great genealogical finds. In recent years, I have had sensational success using Google to find information about my ancestors in the most intriguing areas.

British boys first names

Note – since you are reading this in English, you'll most likely recognize many English names on certificates. Below are a number of English names that have…gone out of style, for the most part, with which you may not be as familiar. Even though you may recognize some names, old English script is difficult to read, so these may assist you in deciphering the names you come across on various documents.

Aberle
Alcott
Aldwyn
Alger
Alvin
Atherton

Beowulf
Bourne
Brenton
Bretton
Bristol
Burl
Calhoun
Cenwig
Chadrick
Clive
Coburn
Cromwell
Darnell
Denham
Denley
Eadric
Gamel
Godric
Halvor
Hamund
Kirkley
Langham
Leighton
Peyton
Radcliff
Sheffield
Thorn

British girls first names
Abelena
Anice

Batilda
Ceola
Cwenhild
Deorwyn
Edith
Elfreda
Elvina
Ethelburh
Fleta
Godelva
Gunilda
Gytha
Heloise
Kinsey
Linsey
Loveday
Marlow
Mercia
Selda
Swete
Utta
Wynnfrith
Zelda

APPENDIX A: IRISH HERITAGE CENTRES

Irish Heritage Centres are somewhat akin to county genealogy societies here in the United States. They are typically busy gathering and making accessible various and sundry records from within their counties. Or perhaps, like individual Family History Libraries for each county. Birth, death, marriage, tax and valuation and applotment records are typical kinds of records you'll find on these sights.

Some of the sights charge a fee for accessing their records. Typically you'll purchase credits, and then each image you view will cost a certain number of credits. They're not exactly cheap, but probably a lot cheaper than trans-Atlantic airfare, hotel and rental car!

My Irish grandmother at 3, 7, and 20 years old.

County	Free Search?	E-mail	Website
Antrim	Y	enquiry@ubf.org.uk	www.ancestryireland.com
Armagh	Y	researcher@armagh.gov.uk	
Carlow	N	dmulligan@carlowcoco.ie	www.carlowcountymuseum.com/carlow-county/st-mullins/
Cavan	Y	cavangenealogy@eircom.net	
Clare	N	clareheritage@eircom.net	www.clareroots.com
Clare	Y	maibox@clarelibrary.ie	www.clarelibrary.ie/eolas/coclare/genealogy/genealog.htm
Cork	N	corkancestry@ireland.com	Cork County Library
Cork	Y	mallowbc@eircom.net	www.mallowheritagecentre.com/
Cork	N	secretary@corkandross.org	RC Diocese
Cork	N	info@skibbheritage.com	www.skibbheritage.com/
Donegal	Y	info@donegalancestry.com	
Down	Y	enquiry@ubf.org.uk	www.ancestryireland.com
Down	N	info@banbridgegenealogy.com	www.banbridgegenealogy.com
Dublin	Y	swordsheritage@eircom.net	
Dublin	Y	cmalone@dlrcoco.ie	
Dublin City	Y	dublinstudies@dublincity.ie	www.dublincity.ie/RecreationandCulture/libraries/Heritage and History/

County	Free Search?	E-mail	Website
Fermanagh	Y	info@irish-world.com	www.irish-world.com
Galway	Y	galwayroots@eircom.net	
Galway	Y	galwayfshwest@eircom.net	
Kerry	N	info@kerrylibrary.ie	www.kerrycolib.ie/
Kildare	Y	kildaregenealogy@iol.ie	
Kilkenny	Y	kilkennyfamilyhistory@rothehouse.com	www.rothehouse.com/
Laois	Y	info@offalyhistory.com	www.irishmidlandsancestry.com
Leitrim	Y	leitrimgenealogy@eircom.net	www.leitrimroots.com
Limerick	Y	research@limerickgenealogy.com	www.limerickgenealogy.com
Londonderry	Y	genealogy@derrycity.gov.uk	
Longford	Y	longroot@iol.ie	
Louth	Y	referencelibrary@louthcoco.ie	
Mayo	Y	northmayo@gmail.com	www.irish-roots.net/mayo/Mayo.htm
Mayo	Y	soumayo@iol.ie	www.irish-roots.net/mayo/Mayo.htm
Mayo	N	westportheritage@eircom.net	Clew Bay Heritage Centre
Meath	Y	meathhc@iol.ie	www.meathroots.com
Monaghan	Y	theomcmahon@eircom.net	

County	Free Search?	E-mail	Website
Offaly (King's)	Y	info@offalyhistory.com	www.irishmidlandsancestry.com
Roscommon	Y	info@roscommonroots.com	www.roscommonroots.com
Sligo	Y	heritagesligo@eircom.net	www.sligoroots.com
Tipperary	Y	tipperarynorthgenealogy@eircom.net	www.tipperarynorth.ie/genealogy
Tipperary	Y	bruboru@combaltas.com	
Tipperary	N	research@tfbr.org	www.tfbr.org
Tyrone	Y	info@irish-world.com	www.irish-world.com
Waterford	Y	mnoc@iol.ie	www.waterford-heritage.ie
Westmeath	Y	dunnasimoate@eircom.net	
Wexford	Y	wexgen@eircom.net	homepage.eircom.net/~yolawexford/genealogy.htm
Wicklow	Y	wfh@eircom.net	www.wicklow.ie/familyhistorycentre

APPENDIX B – IRISH SURNAMES & ANCESTRAL HOME COUNTIES

Sometimes it helps if you can identify an area to begin your research. If all your efforts to locate the place of your ancestor's birth fall short, you may be interested in the list I have added below. It is a list of common Irish names and their traditional ancestral home counties.

If your name isn't listed below, don't despair (certainly don't be offended!). It is simply not possible to list every Irish surname; however, there are several books available that may shed additional light on your search. The first, *Irish Family Names* (W. W. Norton & Company, Inc., New York, NY 1982) by Brian de Breffny is an excellent listing of many Irish names and their counties of origin. *The Surnames of Ireland* (Irish Academic Press Limited, Blackrock, Co. Dublin) by Edward MacLysaght is also an excellent tool for genealogists. Both are well-researched and list hundreds of Irish names and the counties from which those Irish families originated. Those surnames chosen for this book are the more common found throughout Ireland and Northern Ireland.

If your name doesn't appear below, add (or remove) a "Mc" or "O'" to (or from) your name. Irish emigrants often anglicized their names by dropping the prefix from their surnames. On the other hand, many Irish families dropped the prefixes while still in the "ould" country, only to their have descendants add the prefix at a later date.

And, in case you're curious, the ten most common Irish surnames are:

1. Murphy
2. Kelly
3. O'Sullivan
4. Walsh
5. Smith*
6. O'Brien
7. Byrne
8. Ryan
9. O'Connor
10. O'Neill

(* — those Smiths are everywhere! Is it true that Adam and Eve's surname was Smith? Or was it Jones?) Those surnames below that are **bolded** are the top 100 surnames in Ireland.

Adair — Co. Antrim
Ahern — Co. Clare, Cork
Barry — Co. Cork,
Bell — Co. Antrim, Derry, Down
Boyd — Co. Antrim, Derry
Boyle — Co. Donegal
Brady — Co. Cavan, Clare
Brennan — Co. Galway, Kerry, Westmeath
Browne — Co. Galway, Limerick, Mayo, Wexford
Buckley — Co. Cork
Burke — Co. Galway, Kildare, Limerick, Mayo
Butler — Co. Carlow, Kilkenny, Laois, Tipperary, Waterford, Wicklow
Burke — Co. Galway, Kildare, Limerick, Mayo
Byrne — Co. Wicklow

Cahill — Co. Galway, Tipperary
Campbell — Co. Antrim, Tyrone
Casey — Co. Cork, Kerry,
Clancy — Co. Leitrim
Clarke – Co. Galway, Donegal
Clinton — Co. Louth
Collins — Co. Limerick
Cullen — Co. Dublin, Kildare, Wexford
Cunningham — Co. Tyrone
Daly — Co. Westmeath
Dennehy — Co. Cork, Kerry
Devenish — Co. Fermanagh
Doherty — Co. Donegal
Donlevy — Co. Tyrone
Donnelly — Co. Donegal, Tyrone
Donovan — Co. Cork, Kilkenny, Limerick
Doyle — Co. Dublin
Duffy — Co. Donegal, Monaghan
Dunne — Co. Laois
Fitzgerald — Co. Cork, Kerry, Limerick
Flanagan — Co. Fermanagh, Mayo, Offaly, Roscommon
Flynn — Co. Co. Antrim, Cork, Kerry, Roscommon
Foley — Co. Waterford
Gallagher — Co. Donegal, Sligo, Tyrone
Gillespie — Co. Antrim, Donegal
Gilligan — Co. Antrim, Derry
Graham — Co. Antrim
Griffin — Co. Clare, Kerry
Grimes — Co. Offaly
Hanratty — Co. Louth
Hart — Co. Limerick, Meath

Hayes – Co. Cork, Clare, Donegal, Tyrone

Healy — Co. Cork, Sligo

Higgins — Co. Sligo, Meath

Hogan — Co. Tipperary

Hughes — Co. Donegal, Meath

Kane — Co. Derry

Keane — Co. Derry, Galway

Kelly — Co. Antrim, Galway

Kennedy — Co. Clare, Wexford

Kenny — Co. Galway, Tyrone

Kilpatrick — Co. Antrim

Lindsay — Co. Tyrone

Lynch — Co. Galway, Tipperary

Lyons — Co. Cork, Galway

Mackenna — Co. Antrim, Armagh, Monaghan, Tyrone

Mackey — Co. Tipperary

MacDermott – Co. Mayo, Roscommon, Sligo

MacDonald — Co. Antrim, Down

MacNamara — Co. Clare

Maguire — Co. Fermanagh

Magee -- Co. Antrim

Maguire — Co. Fermanagh

Maher — Co. Tipperary

Malone — Co. Offaly, Westmeath

Malony — Co. Tipperary

Martin — Co. Tyrone

McCarthy — Co. Cork, Tipperary

McClelland — Co. Donegal

McClure — Co. Antrim

McCollough — Co. Antrim

McDermott — Co. Roscommon, Sligo

McDonnell — Co. Antrim, Clare
McGillicuddy — Co. Kerry
McGilligan — Co. Antrim, Derry
McGinty — Co. Donegal
McGonigle — Co. Derry, Donegal
McGrath — Co. Donegal, Fermanagh
McGuire — Co. Fermanagh
McIlroy — Co. Antrim, Tyrone
McLoughlin — Co. Derry, Donegal
McMahon — Co. Clare, Monaghan
McNamara — Co. Clare
McNulty — Co. Donegal, Mayo
McQuillan — Co. Antrim
McSweeney — Co. Cork, Donegal
Meagher — Co. Tipperary
Moore — Co. Kerry
Moran — Co. Galway, Kerry
Mulcahy — Co. Cork, Limerick
Mulligan — Co. Donegal
Mullins — Co. Clare
Mulrooney — Co. Galway, Fermanagh
Murphy — Co. Cork, Donegal, Mayo
Murray — Co. Roscommon
Nolan — Co. Carlow
O'Boyle — Co. Donegal
O'Brien — Co. Clare, Limerick
O'Callaghan — Co. Clare, Cork
O'Connell — Co. Kerry
O'Connor — Co. Kildare
O'Doherty — Co. Donegal
O'Dell — Co. Limerick

O'Donnell — **Co. Donegal, Galway**

O'Duffy — Co. Donegal

O'Dwyer — **Co. Tipperary**

O'Farrell — **Co. Longford**

O'Hara — Co. Antrim, Derry

O'Hare — Co. Armagh, Down

O'Leary — **Co. Cork**

O'Mahony — **Co. Cork, Kerry**

O'Malley — Co. Mayo

O'Mulcahy — Co. Tipperary

O'Neill — Co. Antrim, Carlow

O'Neill — **Co. Clare, Donegal**

O'Quinlan — Co. Kerry, Tipperary

O'Regan — Co. Cork, Laois, Meath

O'Reilly — **Co. Cavan, Meath**

O'Rourke — Co. Leitrim

O'Shaughnessy — Co. Galway

O'Shea — **Co. Kerry, Tipperary**

O'Sheehan — Co. Limerick

O'Sullivan — **Co. Cork, Kerry**

O'Toole — Co. Kildare, Wicklow

Phillips — Co. Kilkenny Mayo

Power — **Co. Waterford**

Quinn — **Co. Antrim, Clare, Derry**

Rafferty — Co. Donegal, Sligo, Tyrone

Regan — **Co. Cork, Laois, Waterford**

Rogers — Co. Armagh, Meath

Rooney — Co. Down

Ryan — **Co. Limerick, Tipperary**

Scott — **Co. Laois**

Shanahan — Co. Clare

Shaw — Co. Cork, Tipperary
Sheehan — Co. Cork, Limerick
Spillane — Co. Cork, Kerry, Sligo
Stewart — Co. Antrim, Down
Sweeney — sCo. Cork, Donegal
Taafe — Co. Louth
Taggart — Co. Antrim
Thompson — Co. Antrim, Cavan, Down
Tierney — Co. Donegal, Mayo
Ventry — Co. Kerry
Walsh — Cork, Mayo, Kilkenny, Waterford, Wexford
Ward — Co. Donegal, Galway
Warren — Co. Monaghan, Wicklow
Whelan – Co. Tipperary, Wexford
White — Co. Down, Limerick
Wilson — Co. Antrim, Cavan, Down
Wilkinson — Co. Donegal
Wylie — Co. Antrim

APPENDIX C – BRITISH COUNTY RECORD OFFICES

Each county office in England is the repository of many of the local county archives for the county. Records may include parish records (birth, baptism, marriage, death, burial), land and taxation records, probate and other records of interest to genealogists. Some have indexes, some do not. When requesting information, be as specific as possible: the type of information you are requesting, names and dates you have available.

Anglesey – *www.ancestor-search.info/CRO-anglesey.htm*

Bedfordshire — *www.ancestor-search.info/CRO-bedfordshire.htm*

Berkshire — *www.ancestor-search.info/CRO-berkshire.html*

Breconshire — *www.ancestor-search.info/CRO-Breconshire.htm*

Buckinghamshire — *www.ancestor-search.info/CRO-Buckinghamshire.htm*

Caernarfonshire — *www.ancestor-search.info/CRO-Breconshire.htm*

Cambridgeshire – *www.ancestor-search.info/CRO-Cambridgeshire.htm*

Cardiganshire — *www.ancestor-search.info/CRO-Cardiganshire.htm*

Carmarthenshire — *www.ancestor-search.info/CRO-Carmarthenshire.htm*

Cheshire — *www.ancestor-search.info/CRO-Cheshire.htm*

Cornwall — *www.ancestor-search.info/CRO-cornwall.htm*

Cumbria — *www.cumbria.gov.uk/archives/familyhistory/default.asp*

Denbighshire — *www.ancestor-search.info/CRO-Denbighshire.htm*

Derbyshire — *www.ancestor-search.info/CRO-derbyshire.htm*

Devon — *www.ancestor-search.info/CRO-derbyshire.htm*

Dorset — *www.ancestor-search.info/CRO-Dorset.htm*

Durham — *www.ancestor-search.info/CRO-durham.html*

Essex — *seax.essexcc.gov.uk/* and *www.ancestor-search.info/CRO-essex.htm*

Flintshire — *www.ancestor-search.info/CRO-Flintshire.htm*

Glamorgan — *www.ancestor-search.info/CRO-Glamorgan.htm*

Gloucestershire — *www.ancestor-search.info/CRO-gloucestershire.htm*

Hampshire — *www.ancestor-search.info/CRO-hampshire.htm*

Herefordshire — *www.herefordshire.gov.uk/archives*

Hertfordshire — *www.ancestor-search.info/CRO-herefordshire.htm*

Huntingdonshire — *www.ancestor-search.info/CRO-Huntingdonshire.htm*

Isle of Wight — *www.isle-of-wight-fhs.co.uk/recoffic.htm*

Kent — *www.ancestor-search.info/CRO-kent.htm*

Lancashire — *www.ancestor-search.info/CRO-Lancashire.htm*

Leicestershire — *www.ancestor-search.info/CRO-Leicestershire.htm*

Lincolnshire — *www.ancestor-search.info/CRO-Lincolnshire.htm*

London — *www.ancestor-search.info/CRO-London.htm*

Manchester — *www.manchester.gov.uk/libraries/arls/*

Merionethshire — *www.ancestor-search.info/CRO-Merionethshire.htm*

Merseyside — *www.warwickshire.gov.uk/web/corporate/pages.nsf/Links/80273BD266719BD980256A10004E8B1A*

Middlesex — *www.ancestor-search.info/CRO-Middlesex.htm*

Monmouthshire — *www.ancestor-search.info/CRO-Monmouthshire.htm*

Montgomeryshire — *www.ancestor-search.info/CRO-Breconshire.htm*

Norfolk — *www.ancestor-search.info/CRO-Norfolk.htm*

Northamptonshire — *www.ancestor-search.info/CRO-Northamptonshire.htm*

Northumberland — *www.ancestor-search.info/CRO-Northumberland.htm*

Nottinghamshire — *www.ancestor-search.info/CRO-Nottinghamshire.htm*

Oxfordshire — *www.ancestor-search.info/CRO-Oxfordshire.htm*

Pembrokeshire — *www.ancestor-search.info/CRO-Pembrokeshire.htm*

Powys — *www.ancestor-search.info/CRO-Breconshire.htm*

Radnorshire — *www.ancestor-search.info/CRO-Breconshire.htm*

Rutland — *www.ancestor-search.info/CRO-Rutland.htm*

Shropshire — *www.ancestor-search.info/CRO-Shropshire.htm*

Somerset — *www.ancestor-search.info/CRO-Somerset.htm*

Staffordshire — *www.ancestor-search.info/CRO-Staffordshire.htm*

Suffolk — *www.ancestor-search.info/CRO-Suffolk.htm*

Surrey — *www.ancestor-search.info/CRO-Surrey.htm*

Sussex — *www.ancestor-search.info/CRO-Sussex.htm*

Warwickshire — *www.ancestor-search.info/CRO-Warwickshire.htm*

Westmoreland — *www.ancestor-search.info/CRO-Westmoreland.htm*

Wiltshire — *www.ancestor-search.info/CRO-Wiltshire.htm*

Worcestershire — *www.ancestor-search.info/CRO-Worcestershire.htm*

Yorkshire (All) – *www.ancestor-search.info/CRO-Yorkshire-All.htm*

Yorkshire (East) — *www.ancestor-search.info/CRO-Yorkshire-East.htm*

Yorkshire (North) — *www.ancestor-search.info/CRO-Yorkshire-North.htm*

Yorkshire (South) — *www.ancestor-search.info/CRO-Yorkshire-South.htm*

Yorkshire (West) — *www.ancestor-search.info/CRO-Yorkshire-West.htm*

INDEX

GENEALOGICAL NOTES

GENEALOGICAL NOTES

COLD SPRING PRESS GENEALOGY BOOKS

Secrets of Tracing Your Ancestors, 5th Edition, $12.95
The Troubleshooter's Guide to Do-It-Yourself Genealogy, 2nd Edition,
$14.95

Quillen's Essentials of Genealogy series offers the following books:
• *Mastering Online Genealogy*, $9.95
• *Mastering Immigration & Naturalization Records*, $9.95
• *Mastering Census & Military Records*, $9.95
• *Tracing Your European Roots*, $11.95
• *Tracing Your Irish & British Roots*, $9.95
• *Mastering Family, Library, & Church Records*, $9.95

All our books available in major bookstores, online booksellers, or
through our website at **www.essentialgenealogy.com**.